Nella Marcus was born in Ireland into a family of doctors and writers, and moved to London in 1960. She has been involved in the music industry for many years, first with a major recording company as Administrator of their international classical programme where she worked with such artists as Dame Joan Sutherland and Luciano Pavarotti, and since 1978, running her own music consultancy business.

She has written articles for several music publications and her first book *Careers in Classical Music* was published in 1985 (Kogan Page). Her other main interest is health care; *Fifty Plus* is her second book and she has also produced an audio cassette with Jane Asher about women's health, and is writing her third book, combining these interests.

OPTIMA

FIFTY PLUS

Nella Marcus

POSITIVE HEALTH GUIDE

First published in 1991 by
Macdonald Optima, a division of
Macdonald & Co. (Publishers) Ltd

A member of Maxwell Macmillan Pergamon Publishing Corporation plc

British Library Cataloguing in Publication Data
Marcus, Nella
  Fifty plus. – (Positive health guide).
  1. Middle age. Personal adjustment
  I. Title   II. series
  305.244

    ISBN 0-356-18838-8

Macdonald & Co. (Publishers) Ltd
Orbit House
1 New Fetter Lane
London EC4A 1AR

Typeset in Times by Leaper & Gard Ltd, Bristol

Printed and bound in Great Britain by
BPCC Hazell Books
Aylesbury, Bucks, England
Member of BPCC Ltd.

CONTENTS

Hey diddle diddle
The cat and the fiddle
The cow jumped over the moon

The little dog laughed
To see such fun
And the dish ran away with the spoon

Traditional

Grow old along with me.
The best is yet to be.

Robert Browning, *Rabbi ben Ezra*
from *Dramatis Personae* (1864)

INTRODUCTION

It can never be too early or too late to start reading books about retirement, for it is the approach to retirement that is so important in terms of attitude and planning. This book is intended to smooth the path, placing signposts along the way and spelling out the facilities available when you arrive. It will tell you about the positive developments which are bubbling away and getting ready to erupt, and which will herald the dawning of a new era for the over-50s. It will demonstrate why this optimism should be reflected in your own perception of yourself and your future, as the older age group becomes the focus of constructive attention as far as the desirable things of life are concerned – health, wealth and happiness. You are entering a new and important period of your life, the Third Age – life after work. Yes, it most definitely does exist.

For most of us, life revolves around job, family, promotion, move, perhaps divorce, another promotion, another family – and all that only constitutes the Second Age. It's all go, it's dynamic, and it brings a structure to our lives. Whatever the trials, the tribulations and the heartache, we are sustained by the momentum of it all, by the satisfaction of a job well done, by pride in seeing our children grow up, and by living life to the full. But suddenly, the years have passed, there's the gold watch, or the golden handshake if you're lucky, and you're retired.

What will your feelings be? Relief? Panic? Understandably, retirement means different things to different people. It's a label which suits some very well, but it has tended to divide those who are from those who are not – however, times have changed.

A 50th, or even a 60th, birthday these days is no longer a

1

time to put on mourning, haul up the drawbridge, cutting off contact with all active life. Neither is it a time to sit in your rocking chair staring at a 'time was' channel and watching flashbacks on the video. There's nothing wrong with looking back, but it must not be done in anger or in sorrow, but with satisfaction at having earned those special years which are now ahead.

This book will illustrate why you have good reason to feel positive about the future. There is a growing awareness on the part of society that, unlike in past times, the older generation now merits attention and is a worthwhile part of society itself, rather than just being described as the folks who live 'over the hill'. People over 50 are being regarded in a new and more positive light, particularly as, for many, their spending power, employment opportunities and active life are all on the increase. Reading this book you will learn why being 50 and over is no longer the beginning of the end, but a time to look forward to a new beginning.

Understandably circumstances play a big part in determining attitudes. In the United Kingdom, out of a population of $57\frac{1}{2}$ million, 10,000 people retire every week, and the effects of demographic developments will mean that over the next few decades there will be an ever greater proportion of older people in the population. At present there are almost $10\frac{1}{2}$ million people over state pensionable age and even more, 17 million, are over 50, accounting for 31 per cent of the population. The UK Government Actuaries Department estimates that by the year 2000 this figure will have increased to 44 per cent. However, by the year 2025 the ratio of workers to pensioners in Britain will have declined from 2.3 national insurance contributors per pensioner to just 1.6. This will pose questions as to the ability of state benefits and services to keep pace with these figures and still ensure that everyone concerned can feel secure about getting a fair slice of the economic cake.

It's reassuring therefore to know that issues affecting the older generation are being looked at in a wider context. All over the European Community the situation is being debated, and many forward-looking proposals are being raised at the European Parliament which, if adopted, will benefit older people in all the member states. These include the level of pensions, standard retirement age, migration rights, and a Eurocard for reciprocal concession rates in exhibitions, theatres and on transport for visitors to member countries. Furthermore

1993 is proposed as the Year of the Elderly, while the 1990 European Year of Tourism included a competition for the most innovative idea amongst operators for holidays specially designed for the not so young.

We can therefore feel confident that the welfare of older people is being examined in a collective light rather than in isolation, and this can only be good news. The bad news is that not all proposals have been welcomed yet by all member countries. But older people have the opportunity, through their MPs, to express their feelings on these issues if they wish; there are some 50 million people over 60 in the European Community, and 50 million tongues wagging can make a very loud noise, while in the UK alone, 17 million votes represent a significant proportion of the electorate.

Already times are much better now for the not so young. For one thing they are no longer the poor relations. The over-60s in the UK represent 21 per cent of the population which, with Denmark and West Germany, is the highest percentage in the European Community. The over-55s account for almost 70 per cent of the country's savings and at least two-fifths of its wealth; the spending power of this group is only slightly less than the top marketing target, the 25–45 age group, and they have fewer financial commitments. Generally, by the time you get to retirement, the mortgage is paid, and there are no longer the heavy expenses of bringing up children. In many cases careful planning will have ensured that pensions and policies are now ready to be cashed in, and there is often a substantial capital sum available through inherited property whose value exceeds all previous expectations. No wonder the marketing people and investment companies are licking their lips and wooing you with all the ardour of a young lover. Some advances will have honourable intentions, and some not, so prudence will be needed before tying any knots.

But money isn't everything. Planning for health must also be seen as a top priority. Here too there are welcome developments. We are all living longer, and we are living at a time of great progress in medicine. Advances in medical science ensure that there is less need now to worry about becoming bent, bowed and bewildered than there was in previous generations. The health of older people is now seen as an important area of medical care, with specialist research departments being set up in teaching hospitals in recognition of this fact. So more of us can anticipate the golden years with far higher prospects of achieving the well-being and mobility which will ensure that the glitter doesn't tarnish.

Grey Power – political power for the over-50s – is something else to look forward to. It is already well established in the United States and parts of Australia. In America, for example, the Grey Panthers, part of the Association of Retired Persons, which has 20 million members, is a powerful force, and proved it when they overturned the Reagan administration's intention to cut the social security budget. In Western Australia there is even a Greypower party which polled 6 per cent of the vote in state elections in 1988 and succeeded in frustrating the Liberals' attempt to take power. In West Germany a new political party has entered the arena – the Greys – which fought in the parliamentary elections in 1990; key policies were pensions, ageism and other relevant issues. So hold up your heads and your voting hands – there is an important part to play, not only on your own behalf but on issues over a broad spectrum.

The future is no longer one of going over the hill and down the other side; it's about climbing a new hill, a gentle slope, an exciting and adventurous one, where there's a lot more living and a lot more loving to do. There's the opportunity to look at your children with pride now that they are beginning to stand on their own two feet, even if they do wobble a bit sometimes. And it's a time to learn a new kind of loving – enjoying the grandchildren, with all the joys and none of the chores. They will love hearing you answer their questions about how life used to be when you were young, your memories unfolding in sharper detail than any video because they are from your life and you lived them. You will become a living encyclopaedia for them.

An up-beat positive view of pre-retirement and retirement will be presented in this book, which will reflect increasingly optimistic current trends. This will enable readers to broaden their perception of themselves and the possibilities for the future through the presentation of up-to-date information on what's happening, and how to get the best out of it, in all those areas which matter. The benefits of being part of an increasingly important age group will be highlighted. At the same time careful consideration will be given to viewing these benefits from the perspectives of good health and freedom from financial worries. And you will be shown how you can help to ease the lives of those who may not have such freedoms.

4

Interviews and guidance from experts will be offered, so that those planning for retirement and those already retired can be pointed in the direction of sound impartial advice. There will be a new look at many of the issues which affect the lifestyles of this important section of society. There will also be a new look at leisure, as the chapters tell of journeys of discovery and re-discovery, sometimes even without leaving your own home, all of which your new-found freedom makes possible.

When you reach that significant birthday, if anyone tells you you are past it, agree. You certainly are. You are past the worry and responsibility of bringing up children. You are past being a slave to the tedium of commuting, and the stresses and strains of the rat race. You are certainly past all that, and you're past the post, winning the race and in many cases laughing all the way to the building society. Even if you can't actually jump over the moon, this book will show you that aiming to do so can be an enriching experience.

1

ATTITUDES

It all starts and ends with your own attitude. Too often, what you see as you is a mirror-image of how you believe others see you. Too often, you are right. So the attitude of society must change in order that the feedback we receive originates from a broad base of fact rather than fiction.

The first attitude that needs to change, therefore, is the idea that stopping work is synonymous with growing old. It's true to say that it's not always easy coming to terms with getting older, so we tend to push it away, like saying someone is 'pushing 50'. The odd grey hair – that's if there's any left at all – the odd line or wrinkle, the twinge when you bend down and then try to get up, all these can send us skulking past our mirrors, wary of standing full frontal – and that's another problem. It's under-standable, then, if some people experience misgivings, even apprehension, when they are faced with the end of their working days; they believe the prospect of growing old has suddenly loomed nearer because of the stereotyped role society has created for them. But people are retiring earlier and younger these days, so it is society's attitude that must change – the term 'growing old' must be re-defined.

The four 'ages' in a person's life are considered to be:
- Childhood and dependency.
- Work and family.
- When work has finished.
- Later years and possibly dependency.

This is a concept demonstrated by Eric Midwinter, Director of the Centre for Policy on Ageing, who says,

> At the Centre, we define the Third Age by status, not by birthdays – merely where people stand in the life cycle and

are at leisure because of two factors. One is that their parenting days are over, and the other is that they have stopped work. But with the decline of work, and with the tightening of childbearing to having a small family within two or three years, many people are getting over their adult chores by their 50s, certainly by 60. So the amount of time in what we call Third and Fourth Age is often equal to the time they have spent in the Second Age in work and family raising.

It's clear therefore that stopping work is no longer an indication of old age.

The media have also created their own stereotypes: there's the elderly pensioner, often despondent and dying of hypothermia; or the marathon runner, performing feats which would tax the strength of a 30 year old. Both are extremes which ignore the reality that most people are generally somewhere in between.

A result of this stereotyping has been that the over-50s have been seen in isolation, and have not only ceased to be in the mainstream of TV advertisements or magazine targets; more importantly they are no longer considered to be in the mainstream of active life, as if they no longer matter. A recent TV survey in the UK showed only 5 per cent of advertisements had older people in major roles, and a 1988 Gallup survey found that half the over-60s surveyed thought manufacturers were not interested in the needs of the elderly.

It is now beginning to be a different story. The sheer numbers that older people represent, not to mention their spending power, has catapulted them on to the main stage of consumerism. The media are now starting to respond to this realisation and are updating themselves accordingly. TV companies are now showing, or are planning to show, programmes specifically aimed at older audiences, and not just for afternoon viewing. It is hoped, too, that they will make programmes not only for, but also about older people, which will be informative and interesting to a wider section of the population. In fact the older age group makes up the bulk of TV audiences, yet the majority of programmes are still targeted at younger viewers. As far as commercial TV and radio are concerned, once the advertisers catch up with reality, the programme makers will have no choice but to respond to the potential of older audiences.

So that's another attitude that will have to change, as it is seen that, far from being a byword for boredom, older people are an active part of society and are a force to be reckoned with. The over-50s are going to be blinking in the unaccustomed glare of the spotlight that is to be trained on them, as they exchange their rags for silks and black ties, and realise that they too can go to the ball.

But life isn't always a ball. A few years ago companies were offering early retirement, nudging older people aside to make way for the young. Now one hears a lot about demographic changes – less young people around, so more work opportunities for older people. Yet in organisations such as Sainsbury's, Marks & Spencer and the Civil Service, the retirement age for executives is still 60. Eric Midwinter looks at it historically:

> The last 20 years have seen a remarkable drop in the number of men working between 60 and 65. It has gone down from over 80 per cent to just under 50 per cent, even though the state retirement age is still 65. Over the last 150 years, the raising of the school leaving age (when traditionally work would have begun), and the lowering of the retirement age (finishing work), is all to do with the amount of work that was available, so it is chiefly governed by technology, longer holidays and less weekend work.

Another view is expressed by Professor Anthea Tinker, Director of the Department of Gerontology at King's College, London, who points out:

> In fact the most dramatic demographic changes have already taken place due to low fertility (below replacement level in the late 1920s, 1930s and from the 1960s), together with increasing life expectancy, and it is these developments which have characterised UK demographic changes in the twentieth century.

It would seem, therefore, that the main reason the proportion of older people is so high in this country is because the proportion of young people is so low. In 1880 the proportion of young to old was 50 per cent young to 5 per cent old. In 1980 it was 30 per cent young to 20 per cent old, and the gap is closing. Everything is relative.

But even though the supply of young people is expected to fall dramatically during the 1990s, if you want to defer your retirement and continue working, or if you start to look for a new job, you could find yourself face to face with ageism, and this is one of the attitudes which is slow to change.

In the United States negative age discrimination is illegal, and there is a strong feeling that this law should be introduced into the United Kingdom. In February 1989 MP Barry Field (Conservative) introduced a Private Member's Bill – Employment Age Discrimination – which sought to declare it unlawful for an advertisement of employment to make age a condition of eligibility, or to specify that applicants of a certain age would be preferred. The Bill made no progress. However, in March 1989, Baroness Phillips introduced a similar Bill – Employment (Age Limits) – in the House of Lords which included the additional areas of training schemes, promotion and retirement. This Bill reached a Third Reading in October 1989 and was passed in the Lords. It was then sent to the Commons but was too late in the session to be pursued. It is hoped that a second version of the Bill may be introduced; in fact the Government have declared they do not feel legislation in this area is necessary, but they may have to bow to the pressure which is gathering momentum in this significant area of 17 million voters.

On the subject of law, attitudes have given way to pressure from the Centre for Policy on Ageing, who believe:

> that the exclusion of the over sixty-fives from jury service on 'grounds of age' was 'ageist', and that this blatant denial of a most ancient and revered right of citizenship, ignoring the wisdom and experience of the older generation, is a tacit relegation in status.

The rules have indeed now been changed to include everyone up to the age of 70 – that's a start – with the privilege of refusal for those between 65 and 70. Jury service can now be an area where many older people can still play an important role, contributing wisdom and judgement gained through experience. Maybe those over 70 will soon be able to exercise their rights as a citizen too. Things do change.

Another myth which has to be exploded is the misuse of the word geriatric, which vies with 'mother-in-law' as one of the most used and abused terms in the field of comedy, conjuring up images of doddering incontinent pathetic old people. Some old people are indeed frail, and some are incontinent, but it's inaccurate to stereotype all older people this way. Geriatric in fact is the word used to describe the medical side of geron-tology, so, understandably, it is to do with illness. But not all old people are chronically ill. A recent government national survey showed that of those aged over 85, 10 per cent were frail; of the others, happily, three-quarters were still able to live in their own homes. This is no justification for complacency about the frail 10 per cent, but it must be seen in perspective.

Gerontology, which is the academic study of ageing and old age, is multi-disciplinary. Apart from illness, it covers a wide range of subjects, including life sciences, electronic and electri-cal engineering – which embrace the telecommunications and monitoring needs of the elderly and disabled people – design for housing, education, geography, laws and theology. The benefits of this multi-disciplinary base have many practical applications. Design for housing encourages a trend towards designing fittings for the home which really are applicable for all age groups. By designing for everyone, you include older people as well; the divisive effect is eliminated, and the idea becomes commercially viable. Much of what may be considered more convenient for older people is in fact more convenient for everyone. For example, who hasn't stubbed their toes stepping out and over the edge of a shower bowl? It makes good sense to eliminate the bowl, tile the floor, and have a large plug-hole under the shower with the levels sloping towards it to take the water. In other countries in Europe this is standard practice, regardless of age. Then there are the electronic monitoring programmes that are used to check heart and pulse rates by remote control. This system is also being used to monitor pregnant women in their homes, so all ages are benefiting. All this is encouraging evidence that some attitudes are changing and that some organisations are working effectively to acceler-ate these changes.

The Age Concern Institute of Gerontology at King's College, University of London, one of several institutes of gerontology in the UK, disseminate their research findings to an audience outside the academic world – to government, the health service and to others through Age Concern. The Institute is receptive to the wishes and needs of the older population, so people now approaching retirement age can feel more secure that their future matters, and not only to themselves.

As we have seen, retirement can cover 20 years or even longer and, like your life before work, it needs planning. It is estimated that in the UK 10,000 people retire every week, yet only little more than 5 per cent receive pre-retirement planning. A report on *Preparation for Retirement*, published by the Council of Europe in 1977, estimated that formal pre-retirement courses reached less than 5 per cent of people approaching retirement. Ten years later research for the European Community showed little headway. And now, into the 1990s, still very little progress has been made.

The Pre-Retirement Association of Great Britain and Northern Ireland (PRA) is a non-profit-making organisation that has been running retirement preparation seminars throughout the country since the mid-1960s. In addition to their own programmes, they run seminars on a day or weekend basis for companies who do not have their own in-house arrangements, and they also have training programmes for pre-retirement education.

Some companies lay on such courses for their staff but, as usual, it is the larger, more innovative companies and the major banks who address this need, many of whom maintain links of continuity with their ex-employees through post-retirement clubs and associations. But change is needed in how far in advance preparation should start – some companies wait until a month before retirement, which is hardly effective where planning in many areas is concerned.

Another change that would be welcomed by many is in the amount of attention paid to the emotional aspects of retirement, as they do not always seem to be addressed with the same emphasis as other subjects. Dr Mary Davies, Director of the PRA, agrees that preparation for retirement should start as early as possible, at least as far as financial planning is concerned. But she is also very aware of the anxieties many people have to deal with:

> When people retire they suffer a lack of self-esteem and feel they are no longer useful and no longer in control of their lives. At the PRA we believe it's very important that we should see retiring people as individuals. When we run seminars, there should be an opportunity for people to work their own way forward. There are different problems for men, for women, and for people of different cultures.

Planning and preparation can influence your own attitude, but it's the attitudes of employers and other decision-makers that also have to be influenced, so that that 5 per cent figure for preparation is increased, and so that their approach to the advice they provide should include not only the important areas of health, finance and home, but also the concept of encouraging older people to be more dynamic and to be more involved with change.

The attitudes of society are changing, not only because of demography, but also because of the work of organisations like the Centre for Policy on Ageing, Age Concern, Help the Aged, institutes of gerontology, and many others, all of whom believe, rightly, that the older age group is composed of first class citizens. Of course it is important to get the practical side sorted out first, but more thought must be given to the personal side too, so that people will be able to examine their own attitudes for the Third Age in a positive way. This will enable them to live and to learn, making good use of their time so that the image in their mirror will reflect someone who is alert and active, not only in body but in mind too, and, most of all, pleased to be at this very special stage of life – the Third Age.

Winston Churchill had the right attitude. When asked how he felt on his 80th birthday, he replied, 'Very well, considering the alternative.'

2

HEALTH

In Genesis the Bible tells us that Methusaleh lived to a ripe old age of 969 years. Some would say, a bit over-ripe perhaps. Then the psalmists tell us that man's allotted lifespan is three score years and ten. However, in primitive societies more than a third died before reaching the age of 20, and the great majority of the rest died between the ages of 20 and 40. When the industrial society developed, better control of disease and higher standards of living ensured that life expectancy at birth tended to be around 60 in the late eighteenth and nineteenth centuries. By 1985 a woman in the United Kingdom could expect to live to 81 and a man to just over 78 years. Clearly, we are all living longer.

In 1988 the number of people over state pensionable age in the United Kingdom was 10,412,500 representing 18.06 per cent of the population. Depending on changes in the pension age in the future, it is expected that there will be an increase of 12 per cent in this age group by the year 2000 – something to think about for those who are now around 50 and who may be wondering if our health service will be able to cope with this increase. At present it is estimated that medical expenditure on the over-65s in the United Kingdom as part of the total health bill is a little over 41 per cent, which compares with over 37 per cent in France and 39 per cent in West Germany. These figures are expected to rise to 58 per cent in the UK by the year 2015, 59 per cent in France and 63 per cent in West Germany.

But it's not only quantity but quality which matters, and our main concern must be to ensure, as far as is possible, that these later years may be enjoyed rather than endured. Preserving good health and fitness is essential.

13

THE HEALTHBANK – INVESTMENT FOR THE FUTURE

The World Health Organisation defines health as 'A state of complete physical, mental and social well-being, and not merely the absence of disease or infirmity.' For most of us this means clarity of mind and mobility of body. Investment for the future in our health, therefore, is just as important, if not more so, as investment in our savings. In the same way, we must find a healthbank which pays the best interest and has the best manager. In fact, your body is the bank; everything in it is valuable. And you yourself are the best manager; you must not mismanage the funds.

It's no use expecting doctors to work miracles if you present them with a body that is neglected and out of condition, hoping that a few pills and a magic wave of the stethoscope will cure all. If you took a car into a garage in that condition the mechanic might well scratch his head, saying doubtfully 'Well, it's your bodywork, you see ...' And at worst you may be told it is only fit for the scrapheap.

Ageing is a process which brings with it the sort of health hazards we hardly thought of when we were young. Some of them are really not very serious but, just the same, they can create anxiety, not least because they are signs that we are getting older. Eyes become weaker, hearing may not be as sharp as before, the hair thins and the body thickens. It can be very hard coming to terms with feeling out of breath when you try to bound up the stairs two at a time as you used to do. Or having to think twice about running for a bus – and then having to endure the sense of shame when you don't catch it. In your younger years these situations may have brought a smile to your lips when you saw them in older people; when you yourself are older, they are no laughing matter.

Worries about more serious health problems are also a feature of getting older. Some, although unfortunately not all, of the more serious complaints are to a certain extent avoidable; heart disease and lung cancer, for instance, head a list of life-threatening conditions which can create havoc even in the early years, never mind the later ones. But by accepting the facts, following the advice of the experts, adopting a moderate approach to exercise and diet, and cutting out smoking, much of this heartache and pain can be avoided, and with not too much effort on our part.

We live in an era of great progress in medicine. Advances in medical research have yielded valuable data on some of the most serious conditions that can affect us and those dear to us, and this data has in turn given rise to advice on how to minimise the risks of and damage from such conditions. So medicine has contributed a great deal to our prospects of well-being. Our contribution must be to use this progress and to plan for the future, so that we have the best chance of preventing many of the medical problems which beset previous generations. We already have proof that vigilance works. For example, very few of those people coming into their 50s now will need to wear false teeth, something which was quite common in previous generations. But where more serious conditions are concerned, even more vigilance is needed; this can be achieved by adopting a balanced prudent approach to diet, drink, smoking and stress – the double Ds and Ss.

HEART DISEASE

Let's keep things simple. Generally speaking, exercise and diet are two of the most significant factors in reducing the risk of some of the more serious illnesses like heart disease. Sometimes, perhaps, one feels that there's too much preaching going on about this subject, and that it can have the effect of overkill. However, this is one sermon which, if heeded, may not reserve you a place in heaven but could help you avoid hell on earth.

When we are young the possibility of a heart attack never really enters our thoughts. But in the United Kingdom we have one of the highest incidences of heart disease in the world – more than 150,000 deaths per year – and it's tragic to think that many of those deaths could have been avoided. It is also depressing to know that, while death rates for this condition have declined appreciably in other countries since the mid-1970s, this is not the case in the UK.

Sometimes it's easier to grasp the dangers which could arise if we understand a little more about how our bodies work. The coronary arteries supply blood to the heart. If they become blocked through obesity, excess cholesterol or for other reasons, the blood supply is affected and this could produce chest pain, maybe only for a few minutes, but more noticeable during exertion or stress. This is called angina, and it is an early warning system. Fortunately, angina responds to medication and a change in lifestyle.

If the blockage of the coronary arteries is severe enough, the blood supply to the heart can be completely cut off by a clot, or thrombosis, or a splitting of the arterial wall, either of which brings on a heart attack. This cannot be prevented, but the risk can be reduced by preventing the 'furring up' of the coronary arteries over the years – through attention to diet, exercise, weight and blood pressure. Indeed, blood pressure is in itself an early warning system, particularly in the case of strokes, which affect the blood supply to the brain and can possibly cause paralysis.

If the symptoms of heart disease do not respond to treatment, surgery may be suggested. This is no longer anything to be alarmed about, although it's natural if it makes you feel rather anxious; however, the advances in heart surgery have been tremendous; during an operation surgeons can now maintain the patient's circulation outside the body, which enables them to work on the heart, or to replace defective arteries with veins taken from the leg, so bypassing the narrowing in the heart arteries in the same way as a bypass road avoids a blockage of traffic in a congested town. The operation usually needs eight to 12 days in hospital, and the patient is expected to return to a fully active life in approximately six to eight weeks.

Sometimes the symptoms of heart disease can become so severe that they result in a heart attack, which can be serious if it is not dealt with quickly – the time factor is very important. But it is not easy to know when you may be experiencing one, and it may not be possible for you to reach your doctor or an ambulance quickly. However technology can now help people who may be vulnerable, with a system called transtelephonic monitoring. Each subscriber is provided with a miniature ECG recorder/transmitter. At the onset of symptoms, such as severe/heavy chest pain, possibly accompanied by a feeling of nausea, the paddles of the recorder are put under the arms and the reading is telephoned to a central number. A doctor there will advise and, if necessary, arrange for an ambulance, talking you through the attack, if that's what it is, while you are waiting.

Trials are now taking place in one part of the country of a similar system which will monitor the heart or respiratory rate of elderly people, without them having to leave their home. Combined with a smoke alarm and panic button, it could call for help and tell emergency services the exact location where they are needed. It is being funded by a local authority and it is hoped that it will soon be available on a wider scale. Another useful device, available from the British Heart Foundation, is a card with diagrams which show what to do with someone who seems to be having a heart attack. If you would like a copy, send an SAE to the BHF.

But whatever technical means may be available, while they are a great help, they are not the complete answer. So, what is? This was a question put to the British Heart Foundation – a charity committed to research to find the causes of heart disease. The reply of their medical experts as to whether heart attacks can be prevented altogether was quite positive: 'Unfortunately, no. We do not yet know all the causes and reasons for heart attacks, so complete protection cannot be guaranteed. However, the risk can be reduced by adopting certain guidelines.'

- Smoking should be avoided (i.e. discontinued or not started). There is excellent evidence that, even though you may have developed angina, those who stop smoking do better than those who do not.
- Blood pressure should be checked and lowered if necessary, then monitored regularly. Treatment by medication is simple and effective, but patients with high blood pressure are also advised to restrict their intake of salt and alcohol.
- Obesity should be avoided – check the appropriate weight for your height and age. High blood pressure is common in overweight people, and successful reduction of weight reduces it.
- Restriction of dietary intake of fat is recommended and foods high in cholesterol should be avoided. Grill your food rather than frying it, and increase your intake of fresh fruit and vegetables.
- Regular physical exercise within the individual's capacity is encouraged, walking and swimming being two appropriate examples.

EXERCISE

It's not always easy to organise regular exercise. Some of us find it a chore, if not a bore. But others positively welcome it, as reflected in the rapidly growing popularity of health clubs, especially with younger people. These people are already storing up dividends for their future and, as role models, are doing the same for their own children.

The facilities available at these health clubs generally include squash or other racquet games, swimming, group exercises and many different exercise machines, so that you can sit on a bike reading the paper or do a bit of on-the-spot running without actually moving any distance at all. And there's no need to knock yourself out by doing too much at a time – over-strenuous effort is never recommended, whether for young or old. Regular moderate exercise can be more beneficial than a sudden intensive splurge to make up for weeks of inactivity.

Health clubs can be expensive for those who are no longer working, but many offer unsocial-hours membership schemes that miss the crowds, e.g. avoiding the periods just before and just after office hours, and that cost far less. Local education authorities also run a variety of classes covering swimming, racquet sports and other sports, all under the heading of physical education.

Other helpful forms of exercise are walking and swimming. Sometimes older does mean wiser, and many senior citizens realise the value of exercise, be it taking the dog for a walk or having their constitutional. Walking brings an added bonus of fresh air; whatever your age, everyone should if possible get out at least once a day, leaving the car at home. Swimming is another beneficial way to get exercise; all parts of the body are involved and it is relaxing.

But whatever form of exercise you choose, the important thing is that it should be regular and enjoyable.

DIET

Walking and swimming, while important in keeping fit, will not significantly help you lose weight. Diet will. The subject of eating and drinking can provoke mixed reactions, ranging from euphoric to violent. For some people food is not just something to keep them going, but a sensual pleasure to be savoured in well regulated doses. Many may now groan as they feel another sermon coming up.

But healthy eating need not mean boring eating, nor does it have to mean a perfectly shaped leaf cut out of a thin slice of lamb, lying in a pool of sauce on a huge plate, with not a potato in sight. For those who like it, this may be one form of healthy eating. For the rest of us, healthy eating is concisely explained

in the Health Education Authority's guidelines:
- Cut down on fat, sugar and salt.
- Eat more fibre-rich foods.
- Eat plenty of fresh fruit and vegetables.
- Go easy on the alcohol.
- Get plenty of variety in what you eat.
- Take plenty of liquids.

For a healthy diet at least 30 grams of fibre per day is recommended; this can come from wholemeal bread, cereals, potatoes, vegetables, fruit and many other items.

Fat in the diet can lead to overweight and obesity, and can build up too much cholesterol in the bloodstream, which in turn appears to increase the risk of heart disease, so reduce fats by avoiding fatty and fried foods. Fats high in monounsaturates and polyunsaturates are much healthier than saturated animal fats. Monounsaturates can be found in olives and olive oil, peanuts and peanut oil and avocados. Polyunsaturates can be found in sunflower, corn, safflower, or soya oils, in special soft margarines, in oily fish like herring and mackerel, and in other foods. *Cholesterol: Reducing Your Risk* by David Symes and the Family Heart Association will give you practical information about cholesterol and tasty recipes (Optima £3.50).

Eating lots of fish is another habit we should get into. Now that we are all travelling abroad more, we're getting to enjoy a much wider variety of fish than ever before. If you want a change from plaice and cod, there are all those 'meatier' fish like monkfish, tuna (not tinned), even shark, and they are all available on the supermarket shelves.

As for most of us, who doesn't like a really good meal with starter, meat and two veg, accompanied by a nice bottle of wine and followed by pudding? That's OK, sometimes, but cut down on the portions and don't go mad with the wine. For some people, their metabolism is such that even regular intake of this kind of menu doesn't make any visible difference to their figure; for others, though, there's the thickening of the waist and the losing battle with last year's wardrobe. Paradoxically, the latter group are the lucky ones because they can see the effects of this kind of eating. Those who can't just go on doing it, not realising that out of sight should not be out of mind, as they store up calories and health problems for themselves.

Fast food chains certainly have their place in our daily lives, but the weak links in this chain are quantity, frequency and quality. Some of us eat too much junk food too often, and the quality is not always nutritious. The sooner we take our diet in hand the better; it's never too early to start saving in the health-bank and storing up those dividends which will be so reassuring in the later years.

A free straightforward *Guide to Healthy Eating* is available from the Health Education Authority (see Useful addresses page 111). There is also a wide variety of tasty recipes to choose from in the book *Easy Cooking for One or Two* by Louise Davies, a nutritionist who has made a study of healthy eating for the not so young (available in Penguin paperback).

SMOKING

It's not only lack of exercise and too much of the wrong foods which can be blamed for heart disease and other serious medical problems. Smoking is another contributory factor. Not forgetting, of course, that smoking is also a proven direct cause of lung cancer, which in the UK claims more lives than any other form of cancer in men, and in women is now the second most prevalent cause of death from cancer. The total number is approximately 40,000 every year.

Understandably, it's difficult for some people to give up smoking. It's far easier not to start at all. But when you are young you feel you want to experiment, or you can't resist the pressures to conform, and then you're hooked. By the time you reach the middle years it's even more difficult to give up. Stress, caused by the pressures of work and the increasing pace of life, can easily give you an excuse to carry on smoking. Beguiling advertisements with their subliminal messages don't help either.

Resist. There's nothing beguiling about lung cancer or heart disease. If you can't give up on your own, ask the advice of your doctor.

ALCOHOL

Alcohol is another subject on which the medical profession have strong feelings. Don't we all, one way or another? Everyone will have read and heard all about the dos and don'ts, the whys and the wherefores as far as drinking is concerned, but if you analyse them all objectively you will see that, apart from specific advice from your doctor regarding any health problems you might have, no one is actually telling you never to have another drink.

That's a relief. But what they are saying is keep the drinking within acceptable limits. According to the Health Education Authority, these limits are no more than 2 or 3 pints of beer (equivalent to four or six units) two or three times per week for men; women should not drink more than two or three units, two or three times a week. The HEA define a unit as being equivalent to half a pint of ordinary beer, or a single measure of spirits, or a small glass of sherry, or one glass of wine. (In Northern Ireland, a single measure of spirits is equal to $1\frac{1}{2}$ units, not 1 unit as in the rest of the UK.) It is also recommended that you don't drink every day – give the body a day off.

This is good news and reflects the feelings of most people, not only because of health reasons but because alcohol can be more enjoyable that way. What could be worse than a hangover the morning after a party at which you threw the cat out the window, and you don't even remember? As for the cat, it was genuine Staffordshire. Smashing time!

STRESS

Stress is another danger area. The trouble with stress is that one adjusts to it – you miss it when you don't have it, so you go on driving yourself on a collision course and, inevitably, you lose control. Different situations can provoke severe stress in different people; some personalities are very vulnerable, some not so much. Very often the accumulation of daily frustrations can trigger off stress, so that you feel yourself tighten all your muscles in an effort to cope. Frustration and anger fuel this fire, which can in turn lead to high blood pressure and, in time, to a heart attack.

It's not easy to change your personality, but you must try to make changes in your lifestyle if you are going to try and avoid the dangers the build-up of stress over the years may bring. For a start, the importance of relaxation cannot be over-emphasised. There is a saying, 'You work hard, you play hard'. If you are still working, 'play' is the crucial word. Hard work can be good for you, but making sure that specific relaxation time is included in your day is also good for you. Workaholics are as much a danger to themselves and those around them as alcoholics – like alcohol, too much work affects your judgement, your family and your health. If you haven't learnt this lesson in your younger years you will be building up an unhealthy overdraft in the healthbank; the last thing you want when you stop work is to be badly in the red as far as your health is concerned, with interest rates way above base rate. None of us can afford that.

PREVENTIVE MEDICINE

But the good news must be remembered too. Because of various advances in medicine, we have a better chance nowadays of avoiding many serious problems, providing vigilance is maintained. This is what preventive medicine is all about; it ensures that if some of these problems do arise, they will have a much better chance of successful treatment through early diagnosis. Preventive medicine is a way of helping us to maintain the quality of life into our later years. By taking some responsibility for our own health, we are doing our best to avoid that unhealthy overdraft.

Women

Men and women experience certain changes in their bodies around the age of 50. For women, the most significant development will be when menstruation ceases, indicating the end of their childbearing years. This is called the menopause. It usually starts around 50 but can happen earlier or later, after a hysterectomy or for other health reasons.

Menstruation is controlled by the hormones oestrogen and progesterone, both of which are produced by the ovaries. As women get older the ovaries cease to produce these hormones and the menstrual cycle stops, sometimes gradually, sometimes suddenly. This fall in hormone levels can produce various other changes in the body; the reproductive organs shrink, there is a loss of elasticity in the skin, dryness of the vagina, and, in some cases, hot flushes, night sweats and other symptoms. Clearly, one cannot ignore these worrying developments that some women experience, but it must be noted that most women will have few if any of them at all. Only about 15 per cent will have severe symptoms and, for many of those who do, treatment may be possible.

HRT (hormone replacement therapy) produces mixed reactions in doctors, and physical reactions in some patients too – it is not suitable for everyone. It replaces the natural hormones that diminish during and after the menopause, and as such it is generally successful in removing many of the disturbing symptoms.

HRT is also considered to be effective in preventing osteoporosis, or brittle bone disease as it's sometimes called. Osteoporosis mostly affects women around the age of 60 and over, though a few men can experience it too in their 70s. One in four women is at risk when they are past the age of 50. Osteoporosis results from a loss of calcium from the body, a process brought about by the fall in the levels of the natural hormone oestrogen that occurs around the menopause; this loss of calcium weakens the bones, and means greater vulnerability to fractures after falls. The vertebrae of the spine can also fracture when they are no longer strong enough to support the body weight; this can result in the loss of height that is sometimes noticeable in older women, or can lead to a spinal deformity known as dowager's hump, where the back is bent over. Most importantly, osteoporosis can be painful and can restrict activity.

HRT replaces the body's natural hormones, in particular oestrogen, and thus reduces or partly reverses the loss of calcium from the bones, leaving them stronger. But, while it is generally accepted within the medical world that HRT is effective in this area, there have been anxieties voiced by some members of the medical profession, who believe that in some instances it may be a contributory factor in the development of breast cancer. Others have refuted this claim, adding that there may be indications that it helps avoid heart disease in some instances, but it looks as if the medical arguments will go on for a long time. The best way to approach the subject is to discuss it with your doctor, who will not only give you an informed opinion but will indicate whether or not it is suitable for you. For younger women there is a test that can be performed around the 30s or 40s that can detect whether or not a particular woman is likely to be vulnerable to osteoporosis later on; this test is not yet widely available, but your GP will be able to advise you. It helps to limit the future risk of osteoporosis if you ensure you get plenty of exercise and physical activity throughout your life.

However you mustn't think that the menopause is bad news; many women welcome the menopause as it has significant advantages. It removes the need for contraception, for example, and indicates a time when the responsibility of rearing a family is generally over, leaving more time for you and your partner. It's important to be aware that while the menopause is another milestone in a woman's life, it is not an illness, and, except in a few severe cases, need not be unduly worrying. A look around you at women in their 50s or 60s, or older, who are youthful in looks and outlook, contributing professionally and as human beings, will convince you that, while the menopause is here to stay, it need not be an unwelcome visitor.

It is true that some women do take a while to come to terms with the psychological implications of the menopause, particularly if they feel it is an indication of ageing which they find difficult to cope with. Talking to other women can remove these worries and enable them to see that, in the majority of cases, the only difference it should make to life is on the plus side. Sometimes it's helpful to go to a menopause support group, details of which can be found at the Women's Health and Reproduction Rights Information Centre or from your local Citizens' Advice Bureau.

Another means by which you can help avoid disturbing medical problems when you are older is to have regular check-ups, either with your doctor or at a well-woman clinic; such regular tests and examinations can often show at an early stage if there is any cause for concern, at a time when successful treatment may be possible.

For example, women are recommended to have regular cervical smear tests, available through the NHS for women aged 20–64, every five years. Your doctor will advise whether you should continue to have tests after the age of 64 and whether, at whatever age, they should be more frequent. These smear tests can detect any abnormality of the cervix of the womb that requires attention so that it should not develop into pre-cancer or cervical cancer. Cancer of the cervix is, in many instances, a preventable disease, and to a large extent it is treatable if diagnosed in the early stages; 90 per cent of women who get cervical cancer have never had a smear test so, although there are approximately 2,000 deaths from this condition each year, many of them could have been avoided.

Mammography – breast screening by X-ray – is available through the NHS for women between 50 and 64 every three years. Again, your doctor will advise if earlier, later or additional screening is recommended. Regular breast examination which you can do yourself is very important, and your doctor, or practice nurse at the surgery or health centre, will show you how, or you can get helpful leaflets from relevant organisations. Again, early detection of any breast abnormality gives a much greater chance of successful treatment. Furthermore, mastectomy (removal of a breast) is no longer considered the only option if an abnormality does occur, so there is now no need for women to be deterred from screening by this understandable fear. If you do find a lump in your breast, or notice any change which is unusual for your breasts, consult your doctor as soon as possible, but remember, nine out of ten lumps are harmless.

Cervical and breast screening are also available through private medicine, and the costs will be reduced if you belong to a private health insurance organisation and you go there for screening if this is part of their programme.

Men

What about men? In these days of equality, do we pay less attention to their health than to women's? There are those who would say that the health of men is very much neglected as far as publicity and awareness are concerned. Traditionally, women have been the fragile ones, the ones most connected with doctors through childbirth, taking the children along for check-ups and generally taking care of that side of family life. But things have changed. Role sharing is growing and men are just as interested and involved as women are in the health of the family – except perhaps when it comes to their own health.

In this also changes are noticeable, and well-man clinics are now beginning to be a feature of surgeries throughout the country. Men can benefit from self examination too, and should be encouraged; such self examination can provide an early warning system for problems which may otherwise be brushed aside, either because of embarrassment, or because of the myths which surround them and which may cause unnecessary concern.

Prostate trouble is something which arises in one in ten men over 60, although generally it need not be too serious if the advice of your doctor is sought as soon as you notice a problem in this area. Very often, however, the whole subject can be an embarrassing and sensitive topic, with the result that there is a reluctance to seek advice about a condition that may be quite harmless but which should be monitored by your doctor.

The prostate gland surrounds the urethra, the tube which

passes urine from the bladder to the penis. As men get older this gland may enlarge, inhibiting the bladder function and choking the flow of urine, which in turn can cause pain. Treatment may involve an operation to remove the prostate, or part of it, relieving the pressure on the bladder and the discomfort which went with it. Generally, treatment should not impair other functions after convalescence.

Cancer of the testes is most common in the 30-ish age group, and is very uncommon in older men. Just the same, regular self examination is recommended as early diagnosis of any abnormality ensures the best chance of successful treatment – 90 per cent of cases are treated successfully.

There is another area which can cause concern, though it is not classed as a serious life-threatening illness. The ageing process can sometimes produce problems for men which are connected with hormone levels. It may not be generally understood, but the male hormone testosterone is produced in decreasing quantities as you get older. The result can occasionally have an effect on your energy and drive, sometimes including the sex drive; this can be worrying and have a disturbing psychological effect, which in turn can trigger off an alarm bell regarding feelings of loss of youth and vigour. Any lessening of the sex drive can strike deep at the heart of the most confident man, and could be very worrying for his partner too, if sex was an important part of their relationship.

Throughout the generations efforts have been made to reverse the ageing process, at least as far as the sex drive was concerned. Jokes about older men taking monkey glands to restore their youth are not funny if you're on the receiving end. In fact the whole thing started as far back as 1889 when Charles Edouard Brown-Séguard, an important French physiologist, announced that he had succeeded in using an injection of testes extract from a monkey to revive his own failing powers – he was then 72. In an address to the Société de Biologie in Paris, he announced, 'everything I had not been able to do or had done badly for several years on account of my advanced age, I am today able to perform most admirably'. He later described in scientific journals how his impotence had gone, and how he had regained better control of his bladder. The monkey gland theory was subsequently debunked, but perhaps it teaches us the importance of mind over matter.

The sexual problems which can arise in men as they get older are genuinely serious, affecting their whole perception of themselves and their role as men. But one should not forget that these problems sometimes affect young men too. Fortunately, only in extreme cases need this become a serious matter, and often specialist counselling can help overcome the problem. Your doctor, whether a man or a woman, will understand if this is bothering you and will be able to advise and reassure you.

ANXIETIES

What of those very serious conditions about which we all have fleeting fears – Alzheimer's disease, Parkinson's and other illnesses which may rob us of our independence of mind and body, and strike at a fundamental requirement for our well-being and mobility in the later years.

It is estimated that 500,000 people suffer from Alzheimer's disease in the United Kingdom. Even one sufferer would be too much, but in a population of over 57 million this represents less than 1 per cent. This is still too large a proportion, but it must be seen in perspective. We must put our faith in the progress of medical research which, if it does not as yet provide a cure for some of these most debilitating of conditions, does at least give hope of advances in controlling these illnesses in the future.

Disablement through arthritis or other crippling conditions, though not life-threatening, could seriously interfere with the quality of your life. Again much is being done in the special research departments which have been set up to make a specific study of the medical aspects of gerontology. This is good news, not only for those in their 70s and 80s and beyond, but also for people approaching retirement who are now in their 50s and 60s, who can rest assured that the future of their health is receiving specialised study and attention.

What about those terminal illnesses, the ones we don't even like to think about let alone talk about, like cancer for instance? There was a time when the word 'cancer' was taboo; it was is if merely saying it would somehow make you catch it. Times have changed. Cancer is now in certain instances a treatable condition, if diagnosed in time; and in some cases it is also a preventable condition. Yet in Britain one in five deaths is due to cancer, which puts it second to heart disease. We have the means to look after ourselves and each other to a large extent – we should be making more use of them.

There is very little we can be sure of in life, and no one has a magic amulet to wear that will protect them from illness. But we must look at our health in a positive and confident way. The Third Age has a lot to offer these days, and will provide even more benefits to look forward to in the future in various ways, but most importantly in the field of health.

YOU AND YOUR DOCTOR

As you get older it is likely you will need your doctor more than in your younger days – go into a GP's surgery anywhere in the country and often there will be more older people there than younger ones. As you get older you become more vulnerable healthwise, and your relationship with your doctor takes on a new importance. Your calls on their time will be greater than before. Very often you will find yourself seeking advice about something which can turn out to be more worrying than actually serious, but you don't know that, do you?

It will help you in your approach to your relationship with your doctor if you remember that they are vulnerable too, no matter what their age. We expect our doctors to be not only professional and efficient, but also caring, considerate human beings with the time to listen to our anxieties about our health and the ability to cure our ills. But under the structure of the National Health Service (NHS), time is something they do not have in great abundance, and they can't perform miracles. What they can and do achieve, however, is their best, and that is very good indeed. Think of your doctor as your friend – not a close friend, perhaps, but one you can rely on. As with all friendships, don't take them for granted and don't put a strain on the friendship by seeking them out about something you know to be a simple problem that will disappear in a day or two. But at the same time don't hesitate to contact them if you are in any doubt.

Private medical insurance is something you may already have, perhaps at a reduced rate, as part of a company group scheme. Some schemes maintain the reduction in rates even when you leave the company. If you don't already have private medical insurance, there are special schemes that you can join even if you are over 65 which provide medical cover under certain conditions. Others operate a two-tier scheme which covers you if you cannot get treatment in an NHS hospital within a certain period, usually six weeks.

For some people private insurance is important, but it's well to remember that while the advantages of not having to wait for treatment is a plus, you may not be covered for long-term or terminal illness. Before joining any scheme, look at the terms and conditions so that you will be fully informed as to what benefits you may expect.

Since April 1990 it has been possible for people over 60 to get a tax allowance on private health insurance subscriptions, whether they are paid by you or by your children for you. However, not all schemes are eligible for this allowance so you should check with your insurer as to whether or not yours qualifies. A leaflet, IR 103, explaining the situation is available from tax offices or the Inland Revenue Public Enquiry Room (see Useful addresses page 111).

COMPLEMENTARY MEDICINE

Much has been heard and written lately about the less orthodox forms of health treatment. The worries of the medical profession, and indeed of many would-be patients, are that the practitioners are insufficiently qualified. But as far as the main therapies are concerned, standards are considered to be high. A directive from the European Commission in Brussels for 1992 is keen that practitioners should have completed three years of higher education in a particular area and hold a diploma in that discipline; a spokesperson for the Parliamentary Group for Alternative Medicine confirms that standards are already high and that this would not present a problem for anyone working within the main areas of acupuncture, chiropractic, homoeopathy, medical herbalism and osteopathy.

For people who would like to consider these and other forms of treatment as an option, but are inhibited by a lack of confidence in the quality of the practitioners, the best way to approach the matter is to contact the Institute of Complementary Medicine. They have an independent register of practitioners, and will be happy to advise and point you in the direction most suitable for your requirements (write to them, enclosing a SAE).

Complementary medicine is not generally covered by the NHS but there are five NHS hospitals in the UK with homoeopathic departments which are part of the Service. Certain referrals may take place within the NHS but it is a grey area, so ask

29

your GP for guidance. Some private medical insurance schemes do cover some of the costs, but you should check with your company. And if you think all this is new and the latest fad, think again; homoeopathy for example has been going strong since the eighteenth century, when it was developed by a German physician Samuel Hahnemann.

Those with experience will tell you that one way to keep youthful and healthy is to be alert, aware, active, and to be interested in learning about what's going on around you, and beyond. At the University of the Third Age (see Chapter 3) they say that when people join them, they stop going to their GP. You live and learn.

3

RELAXATION AND LEISURE

Do you remember the end of term when you were at school, with the holidays stretching out over the weeks ahead? Do you recall the relief you felt, and the carefree way you threw your cap or scarf up into the air, cheered, and looked forward gleefully to the lazy empty weeks ahead?

It was much the same, wasn't it, through your working years? Holidays were those precious oases dotted around here and there throughout the year, renewing and refreshing you after the long months of work since the last one. Leisure time then was prepared for with care and attention, generally built around the family, and you made the most of it before you had to go back to work. The only problem again was that it was all too short.

When you retire and every day of every year can be leisure time, how will you feel? Perhaps most people will throw their caps and scarves up in the air and shout 'hurrah', just as they did in their schooldays. They will probably see an endless stretch of not having to do anything, for the first time in their lives, except that this time there's no work waiting to call you back and shatter your dream. It will be a novelty and a delight. But when the novelty has worn off, will you still be delighted? Some people will – that's all right. But others may have misgivings.

The dictionary tells us that the word leisure means 'free time at one's own disposal'. For people whose working life has, of necessity, been structured to a routine, suddenly having 'free time at one's own disposal' can produce very mixed feelings. Some will make straight for brochures of travel, courses, and

31

other leisure activities, wondering how in the world they ever had time for work. Others may find the loss of structure hard to get used to and the deployment of one's own leisure time a problem rather than a pleasure.

Adjusting to leisure sounds easy in theory – 'if only ...' we have often been heard to plead. But finding yourself suddenly confronted with your wish granted can be daunting. Like the child let loose in the sweet shop, you just don't know where to begin. So, however much of a dream leisure may have been, in reality it needs organising and planning to get the best out of it. Making good use of leisure time is now more important than ever before, because there's more of it. People are stopping work at an earlier age and living longer active lives. This is a new phenomenon; it is only relatively recently that retirement has begun to represent a significant portion of our lives, up to 20 and even 30 years, almost as much as our working lives. In practice, therefore, adjusting to this is not as easy as it sounds.

So just think for a moment. You wouldn't expect to start your career – a vitally important part of your life – without study, training and preparation. The same applies to leisure in retirement, another very important part of your life. Pre-retirement advice will help, and for those fortunate enough to work for a company that provides it, they will find that the seminars include the subject of leisure, and how to approach it happily and constructively. For those who do not have this provided, the Pre-Retirement Association run courses for small groups of individuals on a daily or week-long basis. Adult education authorities also offer courses in many areas of the country, as do other organisations.

Over 10,000 people retire each week in the UK, yet it is estimated that as few as about 5 per cent receive pre-retirement planning preparation. So what about the other 95 per cent? It's not only in the areas of finance and other important issues that planning is essential. For those who already have hobbies or who are passionately interested in one subject or another, there's no problem – they are the lucky ones. But for everyone else whose work has not left the time or even the inclination to become involved in anything else, and who would now like to do so, there's a wealth of choice. Where do you start, though?

Perhaps the best advice for the period immediately your retirement begins is to give yourself time to take stock. The whole business of suddenly finding yourself without a work routine will take some getting used to. So will all those well-meaning friends and family who will be throwing so many suggestions at you. Sometimes children panic and feel a parent who has just started retirement may not have the ability to assess the situation, to think things out for themselves, forgetting that up to a week or so ago they may have been a respected decision-maker in a high-level job.

But while you are taking stock, beware the attractions of 'in-house' entertainment. TV of course can be tremendously compelling, with its day-long range of programmes, many of them informative and entertaining. And as the years go by there will be more and more channels to choose from. But it has been found that retired people watch 37 hours of TV every week. Some would say that's a lot; taken to extremes, it can mean that you don't get out very much, and while your home may be your castle, it shouldn't become your fortress.

SOCIALISING

For most of us, the solitary life is neither desirable nor enjoyable. Man is a gregarious animal, needing contact with other human beings, preferably on a day-to-day basis. The network of human contact in society should exist on many levels to achieve a balanced, stable feeling of participating fully in life. It's good to be affected and tested by experiences outside our own existence in, and perception of, the world around us. This is especially important for people who are on their own. For partners, too, sharing or discussing new interests, contacts and friends can happily replace the gossip about work and colleagues.

When it comes to socialising, it depends really on what your tastes and interests are, how much money you have to spend, and whether you have someone to share your leisure hours with. As you get older, it's harder to make new friends – everyone gets a bit set in their ways – so you will probably find that those tried and trusted friends of long standing, of about your own age and with similar backgrounds and shared experiences, will be the ones you are happy spending time with. However, don't resist meeting new people if you get the chance. Hearing about their experiences and backgrounds and telling them about yours, can replace a dimension in your life which you lost when you left work and colleagues.

If you're good at joining in, you will enjoy and be welcomed at clubs and social organisations where your interests and enthusiasms can be discussed and shared with like-minded people. You may have belonged to some before you stopped work – perhaps the local golf club. Your new-found leisure means you can devote more time to them, perhaps taking on a more active part in the administration, or helping out with events. If you were good at motivating people at work, this will be immensely valuable in the social scene. There's ample opportunity for innovation and organisation if you want to initiate it.

Many of those companies which offer pre-retirement planning also keep in touch with their ex-employees, encouraging them to run their own groups in different parts of the country and sometimes getting them all together for a reunion. Meanwhile, these groups organise their own outings to theatres, stately homes, or whatever the members choose. Apart from the conviviality these gatherings provide, there is the practical benefit of substantial reductions in cost for groups.

But you don't need to have been attached to a particular company to enjoy the fun and the benefits. Anyone who gets a group together can do this; go to the local travel agent, who will be delighted to help with suggestions and arrangements, and don't forget to ask for concession rates. Some of us are born organisers and some are delighted to have the business of it taken off our hands. So don't let those motivating skills you had at work disappear; there are plenty of outlets for them.

Then there are those clubs that don't always have meeting places but which, because of their substantial membership, are able to offer attractive concessions on insurance and shopping. They also arrange outings at reduced cost; one of those recently formed is initiating dance groups and social events throughout the country. All these clubs keep in touch with members through a regular magazine sent to you by post. They cater for people planning retirement, from 50 upwards, and for those already retired. Their style is smart, up-beat and forward looking.

Sometimes people just don't know what is available in or near their area as far as entertainments are concerned. You will certainly get help from the travel agent in this respect, but if you want to discover them for yourself, the English Tourist Board and those of Wales and Scotland will unfold the variety of entertaining events which are on offer. If you haven't romped and revelled at an authentic Elizabethan feast then, believe me, you haven't lived.

For those who prefer the calmer shores, there is a wealth of variety where the arts are concerned. Just think of your favourite recreation, whether looking or listening or both. The major national art collections, the larger opera houses, all have organisations called 'Friends of ...'. Becoming a member is not so expensive and can be good value, as entrance to selected exhibitions is often included. Most of these galleries and museums have a tantalising selection of lectures, guided tours of exhibitions with experts, sometimes after normal opening hours, so that you can see the exhibits in comfort. Or, if opera is your passion, membership of the 'Friends of ...' often includes admission to final rehearsals of major new productions; as you may have to take out a mortgage these days to afford a seat, that's a consideration. Again, there are lectures by experts, and sometimes receptions where you may be able to brush shoulders with your favourite *diva* or *heldentenor*.

HOBBIES

Somehow 'hobby' doesn't seem quite the right word for an occupation that you may be approaching as a serious – or even not so serious – interest to replace some of the hours you spent at work. But the word implies no disrespect. On the contrary, if you become proficient at whatever pursuit you choose, you will be respected by others. Even if you simply derive some enjoyment from it, then you will feel rather pleased with yourself, and that's very important.

The challenge of taking up new interests, or being able to spend more time on the old ones, will be a joy to those who have just been waiting for the time and opportunity to do so. We all need hobbies, as a relaxation from work, to clear the mind and refresh it, to broaden our outlook, to spend our time constructively and pleasurably, to use our leisure time well – I could go on, but do we need reasons?

So when you have had some while taking stock, maybe catching up with waiting jobs around the home, and you begin to find you have more leisure than jobs, it's decision time. The choice of things to do, new skills to learn, studies to take up is vast. It's best to make a list, putting down on paper, or on the computer screen, those occupations you feel could become the basis of a 'leisure plan'. Decide if you want to concentrate on information, entertainment or activity – and there's no reason why there shouldn't be a combination of all three.

Then make two lists. One will have your current interests and hobbies; the other will have something new you had always thought of doing but never had time for, like studying for a degree, or learning about antiques, perhaps even learning to fly. The benefits extend beyond the subjects themselves if the learning process brings you into contact with other people; so choose from a vast range of activities, from the mundane to the exotic, the sedentary to the active, and even the bizarre, like the person who carves enormous totem poles – in the UK! There's knitting and night clubbing, gliding and golf, tatting and taxidermy, clowning, juggling (some of us feel we do that all the time) ... trampolining? Unless you are already an expert at any or all of these subjects, there are classes covering them, and many others, listed in your local education institute guide which usually comes out during the summer – courses start in September. This book is a source of rich pickings, conjuring up skills and knowledge you finally have time to explore. Socialising in this environment can be helpful to those who find it difficult to make new friends. Everyone is in the same boat and comparing notes after class leaves no room for shyness. Courses are also available at the departments of extra-mural studies of many of the country's universities, usually run during evenings and vacations.

Many people will already have established themselves as devotees of a particular pursuit, but for those who are still fancy free it really is a case of choosing a little bit of what you fancy. But before you get carried away, settle down and get a few priorities sorted out. Do you want your hobby to be indoor or outdoor? People lead so much more active lives nowadays that many will plump for sports-oriented activities, either as a participant or spectator. The participatory sports, of course, will help to keep you fit. The Sports Council publish a booklet called *50 Plus – All To Play For*, giving useful information on the options available, and it is available free from the Sports Council (see Useful addresses on page 114).

Some hobbies can be expensive, but if your budget allows you can indulge in the most exotic of pursuits. Learning to fly may be a long-cherished ambition at the top of your list for 'things to do when I have time'. Well, now you have the time – go ahead and try it. There is no upper age limit, providing you pass the medical certificate for fitness, the frequency of these medical tests for light aircraft and helicopters being age 40–50

36

every two years, 50–70 every year and over 70 every six months. Gliding and mono-gliding will lift your spirits as you soar like a bird, and medical requirements here are different – details from the British Gliding Association (see Useful addresses page 113).

If you long for the thrill and tingle of wind and spray teasing your skin, wind surfing is a sport which has its own organisation, with special sections for the over-35, over-50 and over-65 age groups. Details can be obtained from SEAVETS (see Useful addresses on page 114).

More gentle pursuits need not be less exciting; for example, researching the history of your home, your town, even your ancestors, can bring out the detective in all of us. Mind you, this can then pose the problem of what to do with all those relations you may dig up. Still, if they have to be dug up, there's no problem really.

Museums offer a rich source of interests to pursue in their departments devoted to all manner of rare and specialised subjects. You now have the time to ponder on what exactly happens underneath the swaddling clothes wound round the ancient Egyptian mummies, if that's what turns you on. And it won't cost you an arm and a leg either. Or there's simply the joy of having time to stand and stare, perhaps at the treasures and paintings which fill the galleries and stately homes throughout the land. This is a heritage to be wondered at. You may wonder too at the puzzling spectacle of some contemporary art which can be seen, free of charge, at many commercial galleries. It is said that serendipity is the facility of making happy and unexpected discoveries by accident; if you go to the right places, serendipity can be yours.

For those for whom learning is a means of relaxation without any pressure to work for a degree, the University of the Third Age is indeed an interest which is informative, entertaining and active. The concept was started in France in 1972 and is now known as Université du Libre Temps (Free Time University). In the UK the U3A, as it's called, is a self-help organisation of people who are no longer in paid work. Small study groups are formed of members who have a common interest in a particular subject; one of the group with some expertise in that subject then acts as co-ordinator, and is responsible for the learning and teaching programme. The wide range of subjects includes languages, economics, bridge, philosophy and local church architecture, and it is all administered through a national network of 15,000 members. Within this structure there are regular Monday morning talks by guest lecturers, where members can get together in larger numbers than the study groups. There is no university campus and no prescribed syllabus; the subjects are chosen by the members themselves, who meet regularly at different venues arranged by their own administration, and where social activities also take place. Travel programmes in the UK and abroad are also available. There is even a telephone group in London for members who are housebound; they 'meet' monthly on a phone link-up for a discussion of a literary work chosen in advance. Fees are very reasonable. For information on groups nationally write to U3A.

Just as there are horses for courses, so there are courses for horses, and when it comes to signing on for a course or to learn more about your favourite hobby it will be difficult to pick the winner. In fact they are all winners, and a glance at a local adult education institute brochure will make you feel spoiled for choice. But be selective and try not to overdo things. You won't be restricted too much by money either, because the concessionary rate for the over-60s brings the cost down to a few pounds in many instances. So take your pick from ceramics or conservation, archaeology or zoology, or any other 'ology'. Then there's Yoruba, which brings us to holidays.

HOLIDAYS

There are holidays where you want to do nothing but lie on a beach, and those where you want to do anything but that. The great plus about holidays when you are no longer working is that you are free to choose when to go away, and can take advantage of low peak periods when the crowds and costs are greatly reduced. Also, you are no longer tied to school holidays so the prospect of queuing behind hundreds of knapsacks, being stared at in museums by hundreds of pairs of young eyes who would rather look at anything than the pictures, mercifully disappears.

All tastes are catered for by an industry which is fast catching up with the fact that travel for the over-50s is becoming a major growth area. Operators in this field are out to please, with some innovative ideas which would challenge people much younger; a glance at the choice available from specialist and non-specialist holiday firms makes it clear that they do not feel they need to make allowances for those who are not so young in years, although less strenuous holidays are also available for those who prefer them. Rail and air travel offer concessionary fares on many routes for senior citizens and their spouses, even if they are younger, so you can travel more for less.

Saga, the holiday company which specialises in holidays for the 'not so young', have recently sponsored a mountaineering expedition for the over-60s, including a climb up a 21,000-foot unclimbed Himalayan peak. It was led by a 66-year-old former Royal Marine, and one of his companions was a 62-year-old who had already successfully tested the effect of his triple-valve surgery at 20,000 feet. A recent Granny Rally to Monte Carlo (entry qualification, over 60) raised £30,000 for International Medical Relief, and also raised alarm amongst the inhabitants of the corniches and the shocked organisers as these intrepid drivers put their feet down and stretched their BMWs and Escorts to the limit, attaining higher and higher speeds in their 1,200-mile drive to the finish, which they all completed.

That's the stuff the young in heart are made of, and anyone who feels daunted by the thought of the years passing or fears the loss of capacity for challenge should remember it. They should also remember that competing is not an essential. There will always be those who enjoy these exceptional activities, but the vast majority may well prefer something less hectic; however, now you have the time to linger and appreciate what you find, any holiday you take can be a challenge of discovery, whatever form it takes.

Furthermore, limiting yourself to the regulation two-to-three-week period is no longer necessary. In fact, many senior citizens on all budgets spend the whole winter abroad in the sun, getting away from the coldest months of the year in the UK. This makes good budgeting sense, as not only are you avoiding the expense of heating bills, but such long-term bookings are also available at substantially reduced prices – they enable hotels to keep their staff on during the winter months when they might otherwise have been forced to close the hotels and lose the staff.

Time-sharing has become very popular in recent years, although it has also attracted much adverse criticism as a result of some aggressive and questionable marketing methods on the part of some operators. At its best it gives you the opportunity to buy the use of a property – a flat or villa perhaps – for an agreed period during each year. This can be for a week or longer. This is an investment which represents a negotiable asset; it can be sold, and in some cases exchanged or sublet, although it must be remembered that, as with any investment, the value can go down as well as up. And there is always the possibility to bear in mind that, if you need or want to sell at a particular time, you may not be able to get back what you paid for it.

To make sure you approach time-sharing with as much prudence as possible, check whether there is a 'cooling off' period before signing any contract; this is sometimes possible with a cancellation fee. Establish clearly what the maintenance fees cover and how the property is managed. Make sure also that the contract enables you to exchange your time-share with anyone else for the period you have contracted. Concern about the methods of marketing and selling time-share schemes have been widespread, and the Office of Fair Trading is now examining the situation with a view to suggesting that a new law be introduced to protect the purchaser. Meanwhile, before signing anything consult a solicitor, and get in touch with the Independent Association of Time-share Owners, a consumer body looking after the interests of purchasers. There is also a special Department of Trade and Industry leaflet *Your Place in the Sun,* available from Citizens Advice Bureaux and trading standards offices of local authorities, or from the Department of Trade and Industry (see Useful addresses on page 113).

Holidays can also be a time for study. What could be better than learning a language in the country itself where you can absorb the flavour and atmosphere within its surroundings and culture? Eurocentres make this possible; this is a non-profit-making organisation with about 20 outlets. They believe the culture and customs of a country are an integral part of learning the language – if you have the time and the money, what could be a more fun way to learn. The courses usually last about 4 weeks and include tuition, accommodation and outings to art galleries and other places of interest. The courses are quite intensive; and although they are not cheap, they are fun, and there is a choice, some of which are specifically geared to the older age group. But you needn't feel you have to be segregated. Some of the courses with mixed age groups benefit old and young alike; the young may envy your experience of communication, and you will probably feel great satisfaction at being able to hold your own.

If you prefer to have your study holiday in the UK, or just

want to test the water on a weekend study course, the variety is very wide. Many hotels run these courses and for many people this is a really good way of having a break – seeing a bit of the countryside, and learning just enough about a subject to decide whether you would like to pursue it in depth at home or elsewhere.

Cruises are a very popular retirement occupation. They evoke images of elegance and well-being on a floating hotel, dining at the Captain's table, and swaying to the rhythm of the ballroom orchestra or disco. They are trouble free as far as getting about is concerned as they take you from one exotic location to another, your floating hotel cutting its way through the ocean with nothing to disturb your view of the horizon. They can be all that and more. The social life on board ship tends to be full and fast with entertainment, deck games, exercise classes and four full meals a day to battle with.

If you prefer a different approach, many cruises specialise in visiting places of archaeological and historical interest, often with guest lecturers on board to prepare you for the wonderful sights you will be taken to see on shore visits. These cruises really are informative, as well as entertaining. Other cruises with lecturers on board specialise in music, and sometimes provide their own resident chamber orchestra with famous performers joining the ship as guest artists at various ports of call. Listening to, let alone performing, Mozart in a force ten gale can add dynamics to the music the composer never intended.

Closer to home, there are tours that visit beautiful gardens here and abroad, many of them enabling you to visit homes, villas and chateaux which are never open to the public. These tours are run by specific organisations for their members, for example, the 'Friends of ...' and several museums.

Or perhaps skiing is your idea of an exciting way to spend a holiday. Some travel agents cater specifically for the over-50s, one of these organisations being called 'Over the Hill' – very inappropriate. And you can always test your capacity for the slopes by trying dry skiing, as there are centres all over the country.

Travel concessions for those over state pension age, and their younger spouses, are available on rail and sea. Certain airlines also offer reduced fares on specific routes, which can represent a substantial saving; QANTAS, the Australian airline, offer this to over-50s and provide an additional package of holiday goodies within the country which are well worth checking at any QANTAS office or travel agent, while El Al, the Israeli airline, have a similar arrangement for over-60s and their spouses, and British Airways offer concessions on many domestic flights, and some European and long-haul destinations. Check individual airlines for other routes.

British Rail have the Senior Citizens' Rail Card for travel within the United Kingdom, with substantial reductions. It costs £16 and is available from most rail stations. For an extra £5 you can also get a Rail Europe card which will entitle you to reductions of between 30 per cent and 50 per cent on rail travel in most European countries (1990 prices). Rail Europe cards are available at selected stations only, or from Victoria or Charing Cross stations in London.

There is one other important thing. If you are alone you may not have the inclination to go on a holiday where everyone else seems to be in couples. You may not like travelling on your own and travelling as part of a special interest group can overcome this problem. Or you may not wish to pay a single room supplement. There are organisations dotted about the country which provide introductions to like-minded people – the fees are generally reasonable. If you hit it off with someone, then you can arrange a holiday together. The local Citizens' Advice Bureau will know of organisations locally, and some of them advertise in the over-50 magazines.

Just to get you back to earth, don't forget to arrange holiday insurance – you may find discount offers in the holiday magazines. And don't forget to check which innoculations you may need if you are travelling outside Europe; MASTA, the Medical Advisory Service to Travellers Abroad, will help you with information about that. They will also provide you with a detailed medical brief about diet, etc., for your particular circumstances and based on your itinerary, for which you will need to fill in a special questionnaire and pay a small fee.

So, your bag is packed, the fridge is defrosted and you have cancelled the milk. Where do you go? The list is endless. Any travel agent will be glad to advise you. Watch the holiday programmes on television and listen to those on radio if you need suggestions. But somehow, it's unlikely you will need any.

STUDYING FOR A DEGREE

Demographic changes are going to have an effect in areas other than employment. Institutions of higher learning, which may well have relied greatly on the fees from a high intake of young students, are beginning to feel the wind of change. It's an ill wind, as they say, but the recipients of the benefits are going to be the older generation, for whom the gates of academe are beginning to open.

Going to university and studying for a degree when you are over 50 is a dream many universities throughout the country will help make come true for you. You are entitled to the same government grant and on the same basis as younger students, assuming you haven't used up your entitlement when you were younger. In some instances you don't need two A levels to be accepted on a course, and a few colleges actually specialise in mature students. Polytechnics which offer similar degree courses may give you a wider choice of venue, and there is likely to be one in or near your own area.

Details of university courses can be obtained from the Universities' Central Council on Admissions, UCCA, who can also tell you which universities offer the subjects you are interested in. Information about polytechnics is available from Polytechnic Central Administration System (see Useful addresses on pages 114–15).

Becoming a full-time student again, or for the first time, when you are well beyond the general student age is a serious commitment which must not be taken lightly. It requires very strong motivation. Apart from the question of your own ability to fit into a working and living environment which will be predominantly young, there's the question of your family to consider, and also the financial implications. As a full-time student, likely to be away from home, you will see much less of your partner, and your children, if they are still at home, for three years. But if you have their wholehearted co-operation, then the experience can be enriching for all of you.

If your thirst for knowledge is strong but you would like to work at your own pace, you could consider taking a degree through the Open University. In 1985 it had 3,000 students over the age of 60, and has been known to have students in their 90s – clearly, in this case it really is never too late. No academic qualifications are necessary for the OU, and in the main it operates through correspondence, supported by TV, radio and cassettes, with some local tutors. Generally there is a short summer-school held each year where you will be in contact with other students. The time taken to get an OU degree depends on you, and the facility of breaking courses up into smaller segments makes this very attractive to people who may find a deadline off-putting. There are also short vocational and general interest courses, and study packs. Fees are reasonable, and in some instances a small contribution may be available from local authorities.

You can also study at home through correspondence courses, and the Council for the Accreditation of Correspondence Colleges have details (see Useful addresses on page 113).

4

RELATIONSHIPS

Relationships are going to take on a new and different importance as you get older. The need for human contact is deeply
ingrained in all of us. It is something we take for granted as we
go through life surrounded by family, friends, colleagues and
sometimes, when the mood takes us to have a party, by those
30 or 40 acquaintances who become our 'closest friends' for an
evening.

The different levels of intensity and importance we experience in our relationships are many and varied, and we need
them all. Usually there will be one relationship which will be
the most important and it will be the foundation for all the
others. But the idea of existing on a desert island with just one
person, no matter how special they may be, is the stuff young
dreams are made of.

Each individual has many facets to their personality. The
more of these facets that are enhanced and complemented by
contact and communication with other people, the more that
individual will sparkle and be enriched. It would be over ideal-
istic to think that one person alone could successfully perform
this mega-task for another.

As you enter the Third Age, relationships take on an added
meaning. You may worry that you are going to feel lonelier as
you get older, stop work and are no longer surrounded by
people as much as before. All those 'work' relationships which
were once taken for granted – the camaraderie of colleagues,
the respect of those junior or even senior to you, even the
grudging respect of rivals – and which contributed to your
confidence and stability, will now, to a large extent, disappear.

But you must look on the positive side. You can now
develop friendships and contacts which before may have been

put on the back burner because you just didn't have time to do so. You will also be able to investigate new friendships through shared interests and activities – much of this is dealt with in Chapter 3. So if it seems that one door is closing, others will certainly be opening. It's a question of a shift in emphasis, and this may be felt most strongly where the family is concerned.

YOUR CHILDREN

Now that you are able to be at home more, you may have been looking forward to spending more time with your children. But by now they may no longer be living at home, so you are going to have to get used to a more adult relationship with them. They will still need you, but may not seem to want to be with you as much as before.

Bringing up a family, despite all the strains and anxieties, affords a very special feeling of companionship and being needed. No matter how many times you may have shouted at your teenage children to turn down the cassette player, or were confronted with young strangers at breakfast as your children's friends came and went, sometimes uninvited and often un-approved, the house is going to seem very quiet when they are not there.

Relationships with one's children can be stormy at the best of times. It may have been hard to accept the fact that children feel a great need to assert themselves and in doing so have rebelled against the care and guidance you tried to give them and with which you sought to protect them. Just the same, the bond between parents and children is one of the strongest emotional ties. You don't really need a video or a photo album to evoke the wonder you felt at those first steps, first words, the pangs of their first schooldays, and all those other special firsts. The images are all there, recorded everlastingly on the micro-fiche of your mind, and are all mixed up with the aching and the joy as they grow up and become adults in their own right.

When they leave home to lead their own lives and learn new skills, parents have to do some learning too. There is no university that can teach you how to adjust to this new situ-ation; there are no polytechnics or adult education courses in how to let go, but this is what all parents have to do sooner or later. If this happens to coincide with stopping work, you could be forgiven for feeling it's all too much. You miss the job, you miss your colleagues, and you miss the children – the silence at home could be shattering at first.

But nature has a way with timing which can be more effective than any precision instrument. After the first impact of loss and the silence of all those empty rooms, aren't you going to feel just a little bit pleased at the peace and quiet; at being able to listen to whatever your kind of music may be; of being able to fall asleep at night without worrying why the children are not back yet, or even whether they are going to come back at all that night? You and your partner can now enjoy the freedom of planning holidays without having to think of their needs, possibly for the first time in your family life. Most importantly, you will be able to take those first steps on the journey of retirement, getting used to the adjustments which will be necessary, without their watchful eyes making you nervous lest you should falter and stumble. The last thing you want just now is to make a fool of yourself in front of them.

As parents, you will both now have to consider the question of fine tuning the balance in your approach to your children. It's a combination of being interested and concerned while increasing the slack on the apron strings. And this is not only a mother's problem; fathers too may be deeply affected by this necessity to let the children get on with it. It's an emotional tug-of-war, for men as much as women, however much they may try to pretend otherwise.

Could it be also that deep down you dread the see-saw effect – while the children are on the 'up' of their lives, seeking out the thrills of the roller-coaster, you as a parent may see yourself as being on the 'down', carefully coasting at ground level on the bumpers? But that really only amounts to negative thinking, and could just possibly be part of your own adjustment process.

Your fears for their future are understandable, perhaps even justified – it can be a jungle out there. But no one can rob them of the basic human need to cut their teeth on life, making their mistakes, perhaps even getting hurt, like a cat needs to tear at a scratching pole to sharpen its claws. Your children may not have nine lives, but be reassured that, generally speaking, they have an in-built early warning system to protect them. After all, it's what you taught them, how you pointed the way, how you circled the landmarks on the map of life and showed them which direction to take at the forks in the road. It's all there, sometimes buried rather deep under layers of their own excitement, confusion, maybe even apprehension for the future of the

47

world – ours and theirs. But you have to hope and rely on the fact that all this will ring like a burglar alarm if the wrong key is put into their car door, and will ensure that they follow the right road, albeit in a vehicle they themselves have constructed.

So another emphasis in relationships will have shifted. You will certainly go on needing your children and they will still need you, but on both counts it will be different. What they need now is for you to let them go – to study, to work, or just to do their own thing which may not be at all what you had planned for them. This is what you may find to be the hardest thing of all to take. You are going to have to avoid being over-protective, over-possessive and overbearing. They are no longer children, they are adults, with all the respect that that implies. It doesn't mean caring any less, just being a little more laid-back about each other. And learning to communicate with your children as adults on a new and relaxed level can be a lot of fun for everybody.

This process may prove more difficult for one-parent families where that parent has taken on the role of father and mother; this in itself may have created an even stronger bond, at least on the part of the parent. One can understand the motivation. One can understand too the need to look upon the child or children as an emotional substitute for a partner who is not there. The 'one' parent may therefore need to adjust more than most when letting go. As a result children may endure feelings of guilt when the time comes for them to leave home and make their own way.

This feeling of guilt can just as easily occur with two-parent families, too, and emphasises the need to develop and maintain wide interests, already mentioned in other chapters, for the time when you as a parent are very much thrown back on your own resources. But you will be looking forward too, and for all parents, however young they may be in years or in spirit, there's going to be the incomparable excitement of grandchildren.

Meanwhile, you may be asking yourself, what are the children going to do for you?

YOUR PARENTS

If they are still alive, what about your own parents? What have you done for them? As you will find when you get over the stage-fright of your new role as a retired person, the question of family and roots will take on a different significance than before. Although you may find that you have less and less in common with your parents as the effects of the generation gap are felt, you are all inextricably bound together by the familiarity, the cosiness and the emotional sense of security roots can give. However these may all be tinged with feelings of apprehension as you see your parents becoming more dependent on you and beginning to need more and more of your time.

Unfortunately, time is not always easy to give – something to bear in mind as a parent yourself. There may be geographical problems, for example; sometimes parents or children move away, so even getting to the conventional Christmas or Easter gathering may put strains on everyone. Lifestyles change, and many people who have busy lives to run do not welcome the need to find time for regular contact with parents. But the lifestyles of many older parents have changed too. Very often they go to warm climates for winter, or their interests may cover a wide range of activities which do not encourage them to be dependent on you for company.

On the whole, though, parents have more time for their children than the other way round. But a breath of fresh air is wafting through the old-fashioned idea of expecting your life to revolve around your children, even when they have grown up, married, and have children of their own. Perhaps you would welcome a change in your own parents' expectations; remember this if you begin to feel your own children are neglecting you. Give them space, not guilt.

Another thing your parents may need if they are getting on in years is looking after, especially if one of them is left on their own. In the UK 58 per cent of women of 70 and over are widows. Ideally, the solution may be to ensure that parents, either together or on their own, should be able to stay in their own homes as long as they wish. If they find it difficult to get out, though, it's important to arrange a rota of visits from family, friends, neighbours and local community services if possible. In this way they can feel cared for, and need not experience feelings of isolation and rejection which many doctors will tell you are often the most disturbing aspects of their situation. Elderly people can sustain a lot of discomfort where their health is concerned, but neglect by their own families is something they find hard to take.

Some people in their retirement may find themselves called on not simply to look after parents but to be carers; 30 per cent of carers in the United Kingdom are in the over-65 age group, and not all of them are women – many of them are men. If the need of parent or parents should turn to one of dependence, can you handle this and the conflicts it may create for you and your partner? If this situation does arise, a lot depends on circumstances, both financial and geographical, and the kind of practical resources you may all be able to draw on. Now is the time to consider exactly where you feel your duty lies and the lengths to which you believe it should go. Whatever the decision, it should be considered in full consultation with your partner and the rest of the family, if some are still young enough to be living at home.

For example, if having a parent or parents living with you seems to be the only thing to do, bear in mind that just because they are family, it doesn't mean that you are all going to get on swimmingly together. If it is going to create tension and un-happiness for them, for you and for the rest of the family, sometimes it's better to be cruel to be kind, and to find an alter-native arrangement.

There are several ideal solutions if circumstances permit. The granny flat is one, and can be of practical advantage to all concerned. Usually this will only apply if you live in a house where it is possible to convert one part of it into a self-contained unit, with its own separate entrance; in this way your parent or parents can feel independent but near help and company if they are required. It will make life easier when domestic problems arise for your parents, like the central heating breaking down, or when the plumbing plays up; you will be there to help sort things out. It means you can avoid the stress and worry that might arise if a parent is hard of hearing and takes minutes to answer the phone instead of seconds. Above all, it can lift a great worry from your shoulders as to your parent's health and well-being. And for the family it can have practical advantages; if your parent makes a financial contribution, it would enable you and your partner to remain in a house which perhaps becomes too big for you when your children leave home.

There are other housing solutions offered in more detail in Chapter 5, but to be suitable they must be seen as ideal by the parent or parents concerned as well as by yourselves, and this is where problems could arise. While older parents very often don't want to be a burden, they don't realise that wanting to stay in the house they lived in for 40 years or more may no longer be a practical proposition, and could create problems for them and for you. At the same time they may be set in their ways, and can be very demanding.

When your parents become old and possibly infirm, you may be called upon to take more responsibility, as you would expect your children to do for you. So in the run up to their later years, if you really don't feel up to having them live with you, you should be trying to persuade them to plan for their future as far as their domestic arrangements are concerned. Much helpful advice is available on suitable options from Age Concern, Help the Aged and other organisations.

Some elderly people are quite happy to go to a residential home, either privately run or under local authority care. There are also voluntary rest homes run by voluntary organisations, or nursing homes where medical supervision and fully qualified nursing are available 24 hours a day. The high cost of purchasing and running these homes is reflected in the charges, which can range from £150 to £400 a week or more (1990 prices). In some cases district health authorities will contribute to the cost for a person who cannot afford it, but on the whole this doesn't represent the total, and the shortfall would have to be found.

The emotional problems which can arise have to be weighed against the benefits of these arrangements. Older people do not take kindly to change and, despite the fact that in some homes it is possible to have some pieces of your own furniture, there can be a lot of resistance to leaving everything and going to live in an unfamiliar environment. Whatever the problems, though, for anyone needing medical supervision or nursing care it could be a wise solution.

However, it's very important that any decision to move a parent or parents into such a home should be approached slowly, very carefully and discussed as early as possible, with no insistence that your parents' home should be disposed of until they are well settled in at their new home. Visits by all of you to prospective homes should be encouraged before any decision is made. Your parents should visit the likely choices more than once, and if one is of particular interest they should be able to meet the staff, inspect the room, find out whether they will be sharing, and if so on what basis. Confirmation should be given that the nursing home is registered. Further information on private nursing homes in the United Kingdom and the Republic of Ireland can be had from the Registered Nursing Homes Association.

It's a tricky subject, but the good news is that older people of this generation have more interests outside the family to occupy them, and are much more independent than before. With the prospect of medical advances improving all the time, fears for the future should be less and less. By the time you yourself get to your 70s and 80s you will have become older and wiser about elderly parents. Your experience with your own parents and their needs, and how you reacted to the problems, should give you an insight in to how your relationship with your own children should be approached in the future and what you can reasonably expect from them when you get older.

Many of us are retiring younger and the best thing we can do for ourselves and our children at that point is to create an independent life that will revolve around our own interests and not around them. This will enable everyone to enjoy a more relaxed relationship, with all the benefits that this will bring. And anyway, we are going to be so excited by our new freedom and the challenges that it brings that we are not going to have much time to worry about the children. Will it last? Will it hell? Just wait until the grandchildren start coming!

GRANDCHILDREN

Like policemen and doctors, grandparents are getting younger and younger, and the extent to which you are able to contribute to the early years of your grandchildren's lives will depend very much on whether you're still working and preparing for retirement, or are actually retired. In the older days the grandmother was very much a matriarch, and grandparents thought they had the right to comment on how the grandchildren should be brought up. But it's not like that now, and the rules are very much the same as your behaviour towards your own grown-up children are concerned – don't try to take over.

Because childbearing and rearing will be old hat to them by this time, some parents tend to forget that parenthood, especially with a first baby, is a uniquely precious development in their children's lives and must be regarded as primarily their preserve to discover and savour. If and when you find yourself in this situation you will undoubtedly be allowed a peep inside this powdery, puffy world of nappies and talc, but don't push too fast, and don't take it as your right to buy the first pram. Your son or daughter may have very special ideas as to what form this should take, and an original large-wheeled wicker-sided perambulator – however valuable – may be farthest from their minds.

This is not to say that your contributions, experience and skills will be ignored. Far from it. If geographically it is possible, you may be called on for advice at any time of the day or night, and your qualifications as a babysitter will of course be in demand. But let your children do the calling, and if they call too often, don't be afraid to say so. Remember that independent life of yours, full of new interests and challenges? Just be careful your children remember it too.

Unfortunately, now that one in three marriages ends in divorce, disrupting the intimacy of the family, not everyone can assume that there will be regular contact with their grandchildren, even though, as part of a broken marriage, they may need you more than ever to bring some sense of continuity and stability to their new situation. Until very recently, grandparents had very few legal rights to access, custody and care of their grandchildren. However The Children Act 1989, which was passed by Parliament in November 1989 and will take effect after autumn 1991, will ensure, amongst other important reforms, that grandparents and others will have the right to apply for a contact order, giving them a legal right to regular access. They will also have the right to ask the court to decide if they have queries about any aspect of their grandchildren's upbringing which seriously concerns them. Advice about access and other problems is available from the National Association of Grandparents (see Useful addresses on page 116).

If all goes well, though, you will hold a unique position in the life of your grandchildren as they grow up and turn to you for answers to questions that their parents – your children – just can't provide. You will come in to your own again as your memories unfold and become chapters of history more vivid for them than any film or video, because you actually lived through them yourself; you will become their living, walking encyclopaedia, and you will get quite a kick out of that. You will be sought out as *confidante* as the youngsters find their tongue and proclaim, as they have all done throughout the ages, 'My parents just don't understand me.' There's no way you can grow old with kids around. They won't let you – another one of the many joys of retirement. And if you are fortunate enough to be able to share this special joy with your partner, you will be doubly enriched.

YOUR PARTNER

The most important person in your life will be your partner, and this relationship will require an extra vigilant approach in retirement in recognition of its very special quality. Understandably, many couples will assume that a smooth relationship before retirement will continue afterwards, as indeed it may well do. But it would be foolish to ignore the adjustments which will have to be made on both sides, and to dismiss the value of making plans together and discussing frankly the issues which are involved. Any plans will affect both of you in the practical and emotional sense, at a time when the settled routine which suited when work, children and career were involved may no longer fit in with your new status. The clearcut objectives and parameters which shaped your lives together in earlier years – careers, family, plans for the children – are now no longer applicable. The structure of your life is changing and a new set of plans will have to be drawn up; be sure that you both contribute to the design.

Sometimes people deal with the major subjects of finance and home successfully and feel other things will take care of themselves. But what may seem trivial to some could turn into a nagging bone of contention for others, spoiling all the other plans which had been so carefully laid.

Take a typical couple. One partner, usually the man, will have had the major part of his adult life bound up with work. Long hours, possibly frequent business trips abroad, will have meant that he will have been out of the house for much of the time. The other partner, usually the woman, will have been at home much more, rearing children, then probably will have gone back to work part-time as they grew up. She will have responded to the need to establish a life of her own, maybe getting more involved with the life of the community, all of which will have added to and complemented her life with her partner. She will have kept herself busy and made good use of her time.

Then, suddenly, the man is retired. He's at home all day. She isn't. When she is, he gets under her feet. He may have interests like golf or something else, but on the whole all he was ever interested in was work, and now he's at a loss. He begins to feel useless and neglected. He may feel she should change her routine to be at home with him more. She doesn't, and perhaps she doesn't welcome having an extra meal to cook – 'I married

54

you for better or worse, but not for lunch.' He feels resentful. Communication suffers, and trouble looms ahead for everyone. If the man had been used to working at home, and his partner went out to work, the same situation could arise, with the sexes reversed.

The example given is of course extreme, but many people will recognise some of themselves in it, and some of their fears. He is not a monster, neither is she. But particularly if one partner retires before the other, the question of adaptability could become of major importance. There will be jockeying for positions – who gives, who takes – so that you could be reminded of the first days of setting up home together. There were adjustments to make then, but you were both younger and more adaptable; it's not so easy now you're older.

Another important aspect to consider could be the contribution a woman may have made to her husband's career. She may well have provided a smooth efficient infrastructure, perhaps also acting as hostess, accompanying him on business trips abroad, and generally being an important link in his corporate chain of office. When he retires, so does she, so that she may also have 'withdrawal symptoms' and adjustments to make on her own account, as well as those as a partnership.

With some couples it may be the woman who retires from a high-powered decision-making career, possibly having combined it with raising a family. Faced with retirement, the prospect of deciding simply what to take off the supermarket shelves may seem empty and bleak compared to the corporate decisions she has been used to making. This is a case where pre-retirement planning in advance could help adjustment, pushing the horizons beyond those of the workplace and out into the land of leisure.

Whatever the problems, the way forward is to maintain open lines of communication at all times. So often we are reluctant to make the first move, to say the first word; we dread making a fool of ourselves or, at worst, rejection. Somehow we shun talking frankly about issues which touch us deeply, fearing to go further than just skimming the surface of our emotional make-up. Perhaps during those busy working years there wasn't any time, or even any need, to do so.

Take sex, for instance. Most couples would agree that in the early years of a relationship words were not a problem; deeds were what mattered, and there was no embarrassment about fulfilling each other's needs unselfconsciously and with pleasure. For many couples this has continued to be the case. For others though, as time passes, pressures of work, bringing up children and running the home probably placed sex as a different priority within the relationship. In some cases leading a full and busy life as a family may have resulted in less need than before for sexual expression. In other cases sex may have become a bit routine, put on the back burner, sometimes petering out over the years, perhaps happily being replaced by the comfort of a relationship within which there were so many other ways of fulfilment. Sometimes, too, one or another partner, or even both, may have felt considerable relief if interest in sex seemed to cool down.

In the later years, though, when pressures let up, when mentally and physically you become more relaxed, you may feel that sex is still important in your relationship. For some people it can represent a meaningful ingredient, sometimes replacing the lack of self-esteem experienced when work is finished and they feel they are no longer in control of their lives. For many people this readjustment presents no problem: for others it can create conflict.

Emotional inhibitions may get in the way, for example. As you get older and stop work you may well experience a sense of loss, and a lack of confidence in how you perceive your role in life. Some people even go through a stage of depression as they try to adjust to so many changes. It may take time for some to be convinced that they still have an important role to play, and that sex could be an important part of it. Remember, you are still a card-carrying paid-up member of the human race.

Or perhaps one partner thought the other was no longer interested, and was content to leave it at that. But now they are confronted with a whole new ball game. We are all creatures of habit and if, for whatever reason, we have got out of the habit of sex then getting back into it may not happen overnight.

There are a lot of myths going around about getting older. One of them is that you are no longer sexually attractive. A lot of it is to do with image, how others see us, even though the important thing is really how you see yourself. This 'image factor' applies to many aspects of retirement, but for some people the sexual image is one of the most sensitive, perhaps because they have been conditioned to believe that older people don't have sex. Myths can be exploded, though, and should be; when the dust has settled you should be able to see clearly that there's no need to worry about what other people think.

Another area which could create difficulties with sex concerns the medical side. As women get older the hormone levels in their body change and this produces certain alterations which contribute to the menopause. This generally occurs in the 40s and 50s, but has been known to happen younger and older depending on circumstances. One of the symptoms of the menopause is a drying up of the vagina, and you don't need a medical textbook to tell you that this can make intercourse uncomfortable. However this can very easily be rectified, and should be regarded as not so much a problem as a minor hiccough in a major part of your life. For example, there are preparations on sale over the counter at chemists and in stores which can relive this dryness through lubrication; alternatively, your GP will tell you about a broader treatment called hormone replacement therapy (HRT), and will advise whether he or she considers it may be suitable for you (see Chapter 2).

Then there are the couples for whom sex was always less important, or for whom it has perhaps become unimportant; they have no need to give it another thought if that's what suits them. However for those for whom sex is meaningful, but who have worries or problems, there should be no feeling of embarrassment about seeking advice. Sex is not the exclusive preserve of younger people, and problems connected with it are not exclusive to older people. This subject is clearly and sensitively dealt with in a most helpful book issued by Age Concern called *Living, Loving and Ageing*. And anyone who would like to get advice and to talk over any aspects of the situation should contact Relate (formerly known as the National Marriage Guidance Council). Happy contented sex is such a fundamentally important element in many relationships that no one should lose a moment's sleep, or a moment's shared pleasure, by embarrassment or reluctance to seek advice about problems, should they arise.

Sex apart, the fact has to be faced that not all relationships continue to be as ideal in the later years as they were in the beginning. Very often couples may have drifted apart over the years and it was only the children that kept them together. Now the children have grown up and left home, the couple may well be faced with a bleak future. When retirement looms and the implications of what that means begin to be understood fully, what exactly do they think about it all? Does it mean a life of domestic boredom and silence, if communication has truly broken down? Does it mean staying together just to keep up appearances, or is it because neither partner knows any other life and is now afraid that it's too late to start building a new one?

In such circumstances retirement may have a different significance – it will be about far more than pensions and hobbies. One way of approaching this situation is to have a very frank discussion putting all your cards on the table. Maybe shuffling the pack again might deal a few jokers this time. You still have some trump cards, like sharing the home, children, maybe grandchildren, friends and social life. That's a start but, if there's so little communication, is it enough? Try to remember what attracted you to each other in the first place; there must have been shared interests then, before the whirlwind of your lives took over and left in its wake a breakdown in communications.

SEPARATION

If you really begin to think of the options open to you, like separating and each going your own way, make sure you realise the implications before you decide on this step. One or both of you may feel the need to have a new life, to shape it differently, to breathe a new stimulus into it; but before you can start re-shaping, just look at the material at your disposal. No matter how attractive you may still be, you will have lived in a very protected environment most of your adult life. It can be very cold out there on your own, and you might feel very out of place and isolated in a world where everyone else seems to have an established emotional structure to their lives, at a time when you are going to find it very difficult to start building a new one.

So if you are thinking of separation, take stock very carefully. Get advice from professionals, because the situation is deeply serious. There are organisations which are geared to helping in an objective and practical way, and will have an understanding approach in helping you to sort out your feelings about yourself, about each other, and about your future, so that, whatever decision you take, you will do so in the full knowledge and understanding of what lies ahead, as far as this is possible.

Losing your partner through separation or divorce can be devastating. True, there can be no comparison with the trauma and desolation of your partner dying (see pages 60–2); but losing a partner through death does at least leave your self-esteem intact, though at the time this will be cold comfort. If you lose a partner because a new man or woman has come into their life, this can undermine your confidence, striking at the very core of your perception of your role and worth as a human being.

When you are no longer young and have had what you thought was a contented relationship for many important years, the idea that someone else – maybe someone younger – can come along and take your place can be quite shattering. That beautiful dream of sharing the later years together will have turned into a nightmare which doesn't finish when you wake up.

What has to be assessed is the actual depth of this new situation. Is it the final fling of someone desperately trying to cling to their youth, or is it more serious? Either way, it's a shattering development. And if it is really serious it can present you with many problems of an important practical nature, as well as the emotional ones. For example, the question of the shared home will create anxiety. If it is the woman who is going to be left alone, has she adequate financial means to carry on without the expectation of sharing her partner's company pension? If it is the man, he could have similar anxieties. These are some of the questions which have to be discussed and answered satisfactorily.

In any situation like this it is very hard to be objective. But however much you may feel embarrassed about discussing it with strangers, you are well advised to do so because they are the only ones who can be objective. You may find it easier if you think of them as professionals – which they are – just as you do with your doctor.

The organisation that will probably be most helpful in the emotional areas is Relate. They have trained counsellors who are experienced in dealing with problems of relationships, and who will be able to advise on an effective approach for your particular situation. They will see people on their own or with their partners. Furthermore, they have 400–500 outlets nationally, so you need not go far to find one; in some directories they will be listed under National Marriage Guidance Council, their previous name. If there is any difficulty about locating them you can contact the head office (see Useful addresses on page 117). For practical advice you can go to your own solicitor, or the Citizens' Advice Bureau in your locality.

Don't under-estimate the helpfulness of family and friends at a time like this. If your children have left home, talk to them – this development will affect them too. But though the support of those near and dear to you will be helpful and necessary, don't expect they can be a substitute for the objective professionals. You need them all.

DEATH OF A PARTNER

There is a finality about death which is awesome. Whether it comes suddenly or there has been a build-up of illness, it can leave you stunned and shaking with the force and implication of its impact. You are flattened, the stuffing is knocked out of you, and you just can't take it all in, maybe because you never really thought it would happen to you just yet. Who does? With the loss of a partner, you feel as if you are losing several people all at the same time – helpmate, friend, lover, mentor – so the shock is multiplied and the impact of it keeps coming back, rolling over you in waves, long after the event itself.

When the time comes to start picking up the fragments of your life, progress may seem very slow. One piece at a time is as much as you can handle. You are not trying to restore just one precious exhibit, but a whole collection, and there will be times when you feel there's no chance of progress.

In due course you will feel ready to face the world, but you may find it seems a very different place now that you are on your own. As has been said before, it's a Noah's Ark society, two by two, and the circle of friends you and your partner socialised with – probably couples like yourself – may well regard you in a different light now that you are unattached. Whether you are a man or a woman you are sometimes going to feel *de trop.*

Some friends may be embarrassed about seeking you out, fearing you will think they are doing so out of pity. You yourself are no longer going to be the life and soul of the party, at least not for a while, so you may feel you are spoiling their enjoyment, putting a damper on things. Death has a strange effect on people outside the family. It's as if talking about it makes them more vulnerable.

Whatever the reason, invitations may not be as plentiful as before. For some people, an unattached person could represent a threat to their own relationship. A flirtatious approach to someone who is already attached can be viewed lightly. But if a

60

man or woman flirts, or is even especially nice to someone who is now unattached, their partner may quite unjustly hear alarm bells ringing, and a friend can become a foe.

If the unattached person is a woman, there is often the assumption that she is 'fair game', and that she will be glad and grateful for a quick cuddle, or more. That may be all right for some, but not for everyone, and it can be upsetting and humiliating to a woman, or to a man, who may still be going through the pangs of loss and is just seeking the company of friends who will understand.

If, as a couple, you were involved in group social activities, like hobbies or special interests, then the remaining partner will have an outlet where they can still feel at ease, and that part of their life can continue when they feel up to it. But if this is not the case, then the prospect of initiating a new social life on your own will seem formidable. Many of the activities mentioned in Chapters 3 and 6, especially those which are work related – voluntary or otherwise – will be a helpful start in the rehabilitation process.

The financial considerations are important to consider, especially where home and income are concerned. Hopefully provision was made in the early years for this eventuality; it should have been part of retirement planning, and dealt with at a time when you were both younger and in a position to be objective. If there has been a joint mortgage, this will have governed the position of the property. If there is a will, the terms will determine your position (dealt with in Chapter 5). There may be pension adjustments to be made, details of benefits to be investigated, and if you have investments it may be necessary to review them if the income of one person is no longer appropriate. You should have a solicitor to help and advise on all practical and legal matters, and if you have grown-up children it is to be hoped that they will help too, steering you through the web of bureaucracy you may now find yourself caught up in.

Other practical considerations will probably be easier to cope with. For example, you may now want to rethink the plans you made for your retirement and which were decided upon as a package for two rather than for one. If you are well and able, you may want to go back to work, possibly part-time. If you haven't been in regular employment, you could consider voluntary work, enrolling as a mature student or perhaps starting a small business from home, though this last option should best be done with a friend, as working at home on your own can be very lonely.

You will probably find it easier to come to terms with your loss if you keep busy and interested in what's going on around you. It will take time to adjust and you may just want to take one day at a time. The most important thing to remember is that big decisions, like giving up your home and moving, should be left until you are emotionally stronger. The immediate aftermath of death is such that no one is really in a fit state to decide on these vital issues.

There is an organisation called CRUSE with over 140 branches all over the UK. It is both an advisory and a social life-support system for the bereaved. It provides counselling, a practical advice service, and will visit you in your home if there is a branch in your locality. They have a wide selection of leaflets relevant to the problems you may have to deal with – property, tax, state benefits and employment possibilities. Local branches organise meetings and outings, where you can talk with people who have experienced what you are going through and have come out the other side.

It won't be easy, and for some it will take longer than others; but the degree to which you will be able to feel you are back to near normal will reflect a renewal in your confidence as an individual, and will be a testament to the worth and strength of the relationship you had.

5

HOME AND FINANCE

There was once a rich cynic who used to say, 'What's the use of happiness – it can't buy money.' The idea of trading in happiness, or even health, for money, is something most of us may have expressed jokingly more than once, saying lightly, 'Oh, I'd do anything for money.'

Some people on pre-retirement courses have expressed the feeling that the most important thing in retirement is in fact money, but this reflects thinking that is still conditioned by the routine of work and receiving payment for it. It's interesting to note that they always qualify this by saying, 'Well, maybe after two years I'll change my mind and think the most important thing will be health.' When it comes to the crunch, while freedom from financial worry is very important when you stop work, retirement should be considered first and foremost from the perspective of good health; there's a wealth of difference between being healthy and poor, and unhealthy and rich, and if we had to choose between them I think we would all have the same answer.

When it comes to planning your finances for the future it's sometimes very difficult to know where to start. It is said that an Englishman's home is his castle. In the UK, where home ownership is one of the highest in the European Community – 68 per cent and expected to rise to 75 per cent by the end of the decade – the home has represented the major financial investment, generally speaking, of our younger years. People who have bought their homes may be in a position to reap the bonanza of a property market which has boomed over recent years.

Some home-owners reach retirement with a property which in many cases is worth as much as 20 to 30 times what they paid for it, depending on when it was bought. Add to this the fact that by the time they reach their 50s or 60s the mortgage will have been paid off, and that many of them will have substantial company pensions and lump sums to invest, and possibly additional savings too. Sometimes they will have inherited property from relatives, which will also have increased in value dramatically. If they choose, they can find themselves on a direct line to life in the fast lane, and they can even pick up £200 as they pass go. It's not for nothing they are being called 'woopies' – well off older people.

But this may not be a reality for everyone. How do you get on that bandwagon if your wagon only has room for a honky-tonk piano? How do you make the best of the means at your disposal? Most importantly, what do you do about the home? Do you stay put, or move to a smaller place? Do you sell up, take the money and run, abroad perhaps? All these are options which need to be considered very carefully, without ever losing sight of the fact that the home is the base upon which a great deal of our life is built, and around which most of it revolves.

TO MOVE OR NOT TO MOVE

That's the question. It can only be answered by considering the circumstances of your finances, your lifestyle, whether or not the children have left, whether you will need an extra room for them or the grandchildren to come and stay, or for friends visiting. Maybe you have always cherished the idea of 'the good life' – getting away from the rat race, living in a village, with all the trappings of rural life. You might find going back to the earth provides a particular kind of fulfilment, and maybe you feel it would bring you more in touch with yourself.

There are many options and there are just as many pitfalls. The idea of moving away from the area where you may have lived for much of your life is not one to be taken lightly. If you, with or without a partner, have lived a social life involving neighbours and friends in the area, then you have to ask yourself is it wise to move to another area at an age when the effort of making new friends is possibly less desirable, and the process certainly more difficult. There is a cosiness about familiar things which responds to a need within us when we are older to be able to accept, and be accepted, without too much effort. This could all change if you move away.

If your home really has become too big, you could consider converting part of it into a self-contained flat for letting, although this does entail a certain amount of expense and responsibility which perhaps you just don't want. Sometimes it's not the size of the property but the condition which is the problem. It's a valuable asset, apart from being your home, so if you decide not to move, it's worth spending some money on essential repairs and maintenance. But if you don't know a reliable builder it's best to ask neighbours if they can recommend anyone; at all costs, avoid the 'cowboys'.

There is an organisation called Care and Repair (Paddington Church Housing Association – see Useful addresses on page 120) which will give impartial advice on building problems to older people. If you are on a strict budget, they will help to seek out grants and loans which may be available; this could be particularly helpful to disabled people, who may have special design requirements. For others, Care and Repair will help get the work organised with a reliable local builder. The service is free, but for those who can afford it a donation would be welcomed.

Another area where money could be well spent concerns the security of your home. Get advice from your local crime prevention officer. This is the time to do the best you can for the sake of your peace of mind in the future.

Many people find the solution is to move to a smaller home – sometimes from a house to a flat – but like everything else, this has advantages and disadvantages. It's quite likely that you would make a reasonable profit from moving to a smaller place, but then there will be the costs of the move itself; depending where you move to, it could well be that you will have to bear the expense of providing the carpets, curtains and other fixtures out of what you may have thought was clear profit, not to mention legal fees and stamp duty on the new property. But if this kind of move can take place while allowing you to remain in the same area, it could well be the practical solution. After all, who wants the bother and responsibility of a large property? It may have been fine when the children were around, and you and your partner had the energy to battle with the forces of maintenance, but will you really miss swopping builders stories with your friends, and dining out on tales, not so much of mystery but of imagination, in thinking even for one second that the missing tiles in the roof would be replaced before the winter?

Of course wherever you go there will be problems of maintenance, but if you move to a smaller house there will be fewer problems and they will be smaller. And if you move to a flat there will be some different problems; you may not have to worry if the roof starts leaking, unless you are living on the top floor of course, but you will have to worry about the service charges which cover leaking roofs, because these problems are the collective responsibility of all those living in the building. And when you are surveying your budgeting plans it must be noted that these service charges will not remain the same. Details of your lease will indicate what percentage of the total charges will be your responsibility, depending on the size of your flat, but the lease cannot forecast the extent of the charges involved, and cannot anticipate the pace or size of increases in the years to come.

The other thing to remember, if you are contemplating moving from a large house to a small one or to a flat, is how you are going to feel about having less space. On the whole most people are very relieved and will look forward to having less stairs, or even no stairs at all, to worry about. If you do your own cleaning, this is important. But you have to consider whether you are the type of person (or people) who will feel cramped in smaller rooms, and whether the reduction of responsibility in a smaller place will compensate for sharing a front door with others – as will be the case in a block of flats or converted house – and putting up with the noise and bother this might involve. If a garden is important to you, remember that it's unlikely you would have one of your own with a flat, though a balcony may be a possibility.

Choosing the right location is very important. For example it's a plus to be within easy walking distance of the shops and public transport; this means you can leave the car at home sometimes and get some exercise. Another consideration is that parking restrictions in the centres of cities and towns are going to get stricter, so you may not be able to rely on the car as much as you used to. You might also want to think about the advantages of being near your children and grandchildren. In the early part of retirement, you are going to be busy and active, but in time you may want to slow down and see more of the family. It's then helpful all round if you are within reasonable popping-in distance, if at all possible.

Then you must give some thought to your lifestyle. Perhaps you liked entertaining on a scale which needed large reception rooms. But if much of your entertaining was connected with your or your partner's work, it's quite likely this will change. If it was purely social, however, and you are planning on continuing it, you must take this into consideration when thinking about a move.

Ideally, for some people, a guest room whether for children or friends is a must. Many people opt for a sofa-bed so that when you don't have guests the room can be an extension of the living area, used as a study or den. Don't forget too that if you move from a big place to a smaller one, you will have to get rid of a lot of furniture, and that will take some planning. You might have considerable difficulty in convincing the children that they ought to squeeze that Jacobean dining table and four chairs plus two carvers into their own premises, which could be anything from a squat to a yuppie flat where the accent is on minimalism. There are always the auction rooms, and may the best price win.

If you do decide to move, it can be traumatic – it's said to be the most stressful part of family life, apart from divorce. The business of dovetailing the sale and purchase of properties is monumentally difficult, even when the market is at its best. Two people who are very important at a time like this are the surveyor and the solicitor, and you shouldn't leave home without them. Their advice is important, especially the solicitor's in the case of leasehold property, where things you never thought of tucked away in the small print can give you a nasty and expensive shock. Who else can understand the nitty gritty of legal terminology?

For those who want to avoid a nervous breakdown, there are property agencies who will find a property and deal with the organisation of moving. They will even arrange for some essential services to be notified of your change of address. Another innovative idea is an Open University course called Living Choices, compiled in conjunction with the Good Housekeeping Institute. It deals with choosing where to live, using space and selecting equipment, and is presented in a compact study pack. It is available from Learning Materials Service Office or from Good Housekeeping.

When you look back on it, moving house never seems as bad as it did at the time, and once it is accomplished you can look forward to an exciting adventure. If you like, and can afford it, now is your opportunity to buy lots of new furniture. This will be a great joy after years of making do because of the children.

It always seemed that they never sat down on a chair or couch like the rest of us, but charged in its direction as if on a collision course, with wear and tear resulting. But do take at least some well-loved pieces from your old home into the new; you will appreciate their associations with your past life and they will fit snugly and gracefully side by side with the new pieces.

MOVING AWAY

Some people dream of moving to a small village in the country, where the view from their house is not blocked by another one across the road. They savour the idea of the change of pace, getting away from the crowds and congestion, to a place where the vegetables are plucked from the garden fresh when needed, rather than sitting primly pre-packed on the supermarket shelf. They can't wait for the deep breathtaking feeling that this is the real life, the only life, and that deciding what fly spray to use on the roses round your door is a much more significant decision than whether or not to advise your company's management board to go public.

We all need dreams, and if this is yours there's no reason why it shouldn't be turned into reality, as long as you keep in mind the fact that dreams have a way of looking different in theory than in practice. The approach to this particular dream should be with your feet firmly on the ground, if it is not to turn into a nightmare.

The advantages, of course, look very tempting. Apart from the gentler pace, the people are gentler too; that is to say they have more time for you and for the good things in life. It might even be easier to lead a healthier life in the country if you leave the car at home sometimes. Walking in the city can be noisy, hard on the feet, polluted and aesthetically unrewarding. Walking in the country can give you the wonderful freedom you feel where there are wide open spaces, with cows grazing in the fields.

You might be one of the many people who, realising well in advance of retirement that this was going to be what they wanted, wisely made the move while they were still working. It may have involved the burden of commuting long distances to and from work, but if you were totally committed to the idea of spending the rest of your life in the country, it would have been worth it. By the time you stop work you will have established yourself as part of the community, made friends, entered into the life of the village, and have been accepted, all of which is very important for your feeling of stability at this time.

But if you are starting cold, so to speak, without even having had a weekend cottage in the location you want to move to, weigh up all the pros and cons before deciding where to build your nest. Do you want to be near a railway station, a motorway, within driving distance of the family? Will you miss the bright lights if you are moving away from a city or large town? Will you need to come up to town to shop, to go to the theatre or exhibitions? Using leisure time well is just as important in the country as anywhere else. All these things should be considered and discussed in making a big decision like this.

Depending on which area you choose, you may well be able to afford a better home for the money you have available than you did in the city. However, there has been a trend in recent years for couples to leave the expensive housing in the cities and to move to rural areas, continuing to commute to the cities for their work. Understandably, this has stretched the commuter belt far beyond its traditional boundaries and has pushed up the price of housing in many of these areas.

Nevertheless, there are still some bargains to be found, but don't forget that the cost of living may be higher in some respects. For instance there may not be the large supermarket or high street chain stores with their competitive pricing that you had become used to in the cities. Transport costs should be investigated too, and if you want to be able to visit the larger centres from time to time, the high cost of rail travel should be borne in mind, although the over-60s will receive reductions through their rail cards.

Just the same, they say you can live on less if you have more to live for; so, go for it, but make sure you have sussed out, not only the land, but the practical considerations well in advance because it's a big adjustment to make. The same considerations apply if you are thinking of moving to somewhere by the sea, which also has attractions for some retired people.

If you are a couple, it's a good idea to think of a time in the future when one of you is left on your own. If you haven't been able to fit into the community as newcomers, you could find yourself even more isolated when you are on your own. Although you will be moving 'to' something, you will also be leaving a way of life which represented some very important years and probably some important friends. But there are many important years left, and if being in the country or by the sea is your way of spending them, good luck.

RETIREMENT HOMES AND SHELTERED ACCOMMODATION

No one knows who dreamed up the idea of retirement homes, but they are now a growth industry. As far as older people themselves are concerned, retirement homes and sheltered accommodation respond to a need many experience as they get older – less responsibility, help at the end of a bell if needed, and security for the future. No matter how active you are now and how much you wish to preserve your independence, there may come a time when you need a degree of supervision and security which a live-in warden can provide.

The changes in family lifestyles have also contributed to the need for this kind of accommodation. At one time the older parents would either be cared for in their children's homes or be living nearby; nowadays, with more women working, and houses and flats getting smaller, this idea may no longer be practical. Older people themselves appreciate their independence while being mindful of the desirability of having help on hand when needed, so it looks as if this new concept of housing is here to stay.

There were 40,000 retirement dwellings in 1985 and the numbers have been increasing ever since, covering a very wide field and with some important and relevant features. For example, you can expect such developments to have a resident warden and a method of responding to individual alarm systems of the residents; this of course is very comforting if you are on your own, as one of the most worrying fears arises when you are feeling ill or needing attention and do not have anyone around.

The question of companionship is another important aspect. Many of these places have communal facilities where you can socialise and have a bit of company if you want it, though not all homes provide this. Many even have recreation facilities, such as a swimming pool or health club. The presence of the latter would probably depend on the size of the development – they can vary in size from small blocks to large complexes incorporating a retirement home and nursing home.

Retirement villages is another idea which is very well established in Sweden and the United States and which is beginning to gain ground and popularity in the UK. One such retirement village is being built in Devon; it is a complex which caters for the different stages of an older person's life – sheltered housing for people who can manage very well on their own, professional staff to help when they can no longer manage, and a nursing home or hospice for illness. This gives a secure community feeling and removes the worry of what to do when you can't manage on your own but don't want to move again. Generally you have to be over 55 to be entitled to buy such a property, and you would also need to be on a relaxed budget as all these advantages do not come cheap – the cost of a small flat in such a setting could well be as much, if not more, than a similar property in an open environment.

It all sounds very idyllic, so what are the snags? Well, they are such that it prompted a Private Member's Bill, after several Members of Parliament had received complaints from constituents who had been the victims of financial burdens they had not anticipated. The Bill did not succeed when it was introduced in April 1988 and will be re-introduced another time. However, it was effective in that it resulted in a code of practice being drawn up by the Housebuilders' Federation to protect prospective purchasers from hidden costs, or unreasonably sudden and large increases of management charges.

There are two areas where dissatisfaction and financial problems have arisen. When someone buys a sheltered home, there are management charges to cover maintenance, repairs and services, as one would expect in any other flat. But with sheltered accommodation they can start quite high, and there is generally no stated limit to the increases which the management organisation is able to initiate. This is now covered in the new code of practice, inasmuch as an annual review of charges and budgets must be presented to the owners, and management must agree to recognise a residents' association if it comprises 51 per cent or more of the purchasers. There is now also a formal complaints procedure although, while it must be welcomed as a start, it has limits as far as enforcement is concerned.

The other area of great concern is the question of re-sale. Generally speaking when you buy a dwelling under one of these schemes there are restricted re-sale conditions; for instance, the property can only be sold back to the management company on terms which may well be at a loss for the owners, perhaps because it was bought at a discount in the first place. Or if it is put on sale on the open market, sometimes a percentage of the sale price has to go to the management company, even if they don't act as agents.

The code of practice covers these points and others, but it applies only to new developments, although previous purchasers of sheltered housing do have some protection under the Landlord and Tenant Act 1987. The code also requires the management companies of these buildings to provide annual audited accounts, and it sets out very clearly what you are entitled to expect from the management, and what your legal rights are. Copies of the code of practice are available from the Building Employers' Federation, and include an information pack covering what you should expect for your service charges, what the duties of a warden are, and recommendations for effective maintenance of emergency alarms. Age Concern produce a concise booklet summarising the main points – *A Buyer's Guide to Sheltered Housing.*

Sometimes you may be tempted to borrow money to pay the annual management charges, and roll up the interest until the property is sold. This is not always recommended and should not be contemplated without first discussing it fully with your legal adviser. There are, however, other forms of borrowing which can be acceptable if they suit your particular circumstances. Some housing schemes enable you to buy at a discount and pay rent on the outstanding sum, having no loss of value when you sell, one such scheme being the Park Housing Association Scheme. There is also the Home and Life Plan, where the property will cost considerably less than the normal purchase price, and gives you a 'life interest', leaving the balance for investment. This is only for people who are not planning to leave the property to anyone when they die, as it then reverts to Home and Life. Again, this is an area where legal advice is essential.

There is thus a new awareness of the need to monitor the sale and running of sheltered accommodation and, as a result, there is a renewed confidence in the system as it is now under a spotlight, which can only benefit the buyer. And although the financial aspects and enforcement of terms may sound complicated, there's a lot to be said for sheltered housing. However, if you are thinking of buying into this kind of accommodation it's as well to do it as soon after 55 or the permitted age as possible, when it's easier to view the terms and conditions in perspective to see if they can be made to work for you.

There are also the emotional considerations to remember. For many older people sheltered accommodation is a haven, enabling them to be amongst their own age group. But for others it could be seen as a ghetto. This is one reason why there is a move to situate some of these developments within an existing community covering all age groups. This would surely be an ideal solution, not only for the older people but for the younger ones too, for whom the presence of an older generation brings a stable feeling of continuity.

The best advice if you are thinking about this is to discuss it in great detail with your partner, your family and your legal adviser. Then it's important to have a frank talk with the management of the property and, if possible, with current residents. There are many companies offering this kind of housing, and the New Homes Marketing Board has a comprehensive list of sheltered housing for sale (see Useful addresses on page 119. Enclose a large SAE).

INCOME FROM YOUR HOME

Some older people who would like more income may be tempted by a scheme called the home-income plan; it is available to people whose minimum age is 65 for men and 69 for women, while in the case of married couples the younger age is taken into account. This option includes mortgage annuity schemes and home reversion schemes; generally speaking they both enable home-owners who do not wish to sell and leave their home to increase their income by taking out a deferred interest loan on a mortgage on the property, the amount depending on the valuation of the property and the age of the owner or owners. No interest is paid but it is saved up until either the owner or surviving partner dies, or until the debt reaches a specified percentage of the valuation, sometimes 50 per cent or 75 per cent, when it has to be repaid.

In cases where there is a steady increase in house prices these schemes might be considered feasible, but the danger is that you could end up with an amount to be repaid which is more than the value of the property – and at a time when you will be much older and in no state to undertake selling and moving, let alone buying, if much of your capital is dissipated. Clearly this is an idea which should be looked into very carefully with a solicitor before even thinking of adopting it.

A home reversion scheme is slightly different, in that you sell all or part of your home but retain the right to live in it for the remainder of your life, while the lump sum you receive is invested in an annuity. Again, seek advice before considering this sort of scheme or, best of all, leave it alone until some kind of standardisation is introduced to protect those who are most vulnerable. It is bad enough when you are young to be faced with having to find a new home and the money to finance it, but when you are not so young it robs you of your security and peace of mind which are so vitally important at a time like this.

RETIRING ABROAD

Who hasn't thought of spending their retirement where the hot sun shines in winter, unlike the dark days of northern Europe when the garden is frostbitten and out of bounds? Who hasn't thought of spending their later years where the temperature is always gentle, the sky is blue and the palm trees sway in the tropical breeze – just like a luxurious desert island? It can be a pensioner's dream, but it needs very careful investigation and planning – and you are going to need more than your eight gramaphone records to make it work.

Perhaps you have family reasons for emigrating. Maybe your children and grandchildren live abroad, and you want to spend your retirement fulfilling all those grandparental aspirations. Or perhaps you have a holiday flat or home abroad and enjoy the lifestyle and the environment. For a start, the formalities have to be considered. As things stand at present, even within the European Community (EC), permission has to be sought from the host country before you can do this, and they will want to be sure you are eligible as far as your finances are concerned. The EC is keen to introduce Rights of Residence in 1992 for those over pension age as part of the Social Security Dimension, but this hasn't happened yet.

Furthermore, taking up residence abroad really means burning your boats as far as certain things are concerned. The financial aspect is something you will of course have taken into account in acquiring a residence abroad, but what many people may not realise is that once you are resident in another country, you are liable to their laws, including the buying of land and property, inheritance, health insurance and finance. It's true that company pensions can be paid abroad quite easily, but you have to make provision so that you are not taxed both in the country you left and in the one you are going to live in; this involves making declarations and dealing with your inspector of taxes in your first country of residence. Reciprocal tax arrangements do exist between the UK and many other countries, but you have to present a certificate to the Inland Revenue confirming that the country you are going to is one of them, and that you are eligible; otherwise you could find your pension a great deal depleted through tax being withheld by the Inland Revenue. Their booklet IR 20, *Resident and Non-resident Liability to UK Tax*, from your local Inland Revenue office will help.

You also need to contact the Department of Social Security about your entitlement to state pension and health insurance – write to the DSS Overseas Branch. As far as your state pension is concerned the UK has agreements with 31 countries which offer reciprocal payment of state pensions, but unfortunately in some of these countries the agreement does not cover the payment of increases in UK state benefits; at present these countries include Australia, Canada, New Zealand and Norway, but there are hopes this may change in the future. What it means at present is that the level of your pension will remain the same as it was at the date of your leaving the UK, and therefore in real terms it will gradually be devalued.

You will be entitled to health insurance on the same basis as that of the country you are going to live in, but it must be remembered that this is unlikely to be as comprehensive in all other countries as it is in the UK. For example, much hardship has been experienced by residents abroad who find that extended and terminal illness is just not supported in the way it is by the UK health service. Furthermore, social services abroad may not be as comprehensive as they are in the UK. The Department of Social Security have booklets SA 29 and NI 38 giving relevant information, which are available from their Overseas Branch.

If you have private health insurance you must check with the insurance company, but generally there are systems whereby you can transfer from a UK scheme to an international scheme. But it's important to check if this covers all or selected hospitals, full refunds for treatment, consultation fees and the scale of insurance payments which, in most cases, increase after age 64.

FINANCE

It's never too early to start organising finances for your retirement. Unfortunately, not everyone realises this so, though pre-retirement seminars give helpful advice, they generally take place during the pre-retirement year, if not a few weeks before retirement itself – too late to enable you to plan a long-term strategy. There are exceptions; for example Marks & Spencer start their retirement planning five years in advance and continue to offer advice in the ensuing years, if needed.

It's not always easy to practise what is preached, though. Even if you do think of retirement well ahead, there may not always be the cash to spare to top up existing investment arrangements or to start new ones. Contributing to the expenses of running a home and family, with prices seeming to rise at an alarming rate, leaves very little to spare. If you do find yourself in this position and retirement is just around the corner, don't panic; you may be under-estimating your expectations and over-estimating the effect the drop in income will have when you stop work.

There are two basic sources of revenue you should be able to rely on: your occupational or company pension, which could be as much as, but no more than, two-thirds of your final earnings; and the state pension, paid at age 60 for women and 65 for men, the value of which will depend on how long you have been contributing. You can even have a forecast worked out for you of what you are likely to receive, including your graduated pension and your state earnings-related pension supplement (SERPS) if these are applicable; contact the Department of Social Security and ask for form BR 19. If you have any other queries on any state benefits to which you may be entitled and which would contribute to your retirement income, your local DSS office or your Citizens' Advice Bureau will have free leaflets and information, or you can make use of the free confidential phone service for questions related to state benefits.

Don't forget that if you are required to retire at an earlier age than the state age, you can claim unemployment benefit if you can show that you have been trying to find work. However, any benefit you receive will be affected by your company pension. And if you retire before the state age, continue paying a stamp so that you will be entitled to sickness benefit. But if you retire at state age get a BR 464, which is a card confirming you are entitled to concessionary rates and acts as a means of identification for this purpose, instead of a pension book. Leaflet NI 230, *Unemployment Benefit and Your Personal Pension* is available from your local DSS office.

It is always helpful to be practical – write down on paper the amounts of your pension and any other sources of income, including building society interest, personal pension, bank or savings interest, dividends from stocks and shares. If there are any policies maturing at this time, the lump sum could be invested to bring in additional income. This applies, too, to any lump sum you may receive when you leave your company; some people use this money to buy an annuity, or perhaps you will have commuted your company pension, i.e. converted some of it into a lump sum, so any income from this should also be included.

Then make another list detailing your expected unavoidable outgoings, such as food, rent, or mortgage (hopefully this will be paid off), Community Charge (poll tax), insurance, heat, light, telephone, TV, car, clothes, tax, a contingency amount for home maintenance, and any other general regular expenses – these figures could be based on figures for previous years. Draw a line under this, and below the line add the desirable, but not strictly essential, expenditure like holidays, gifts, books and papers, entertainment and whatever else you would like for your chosen lifestyle.

Generally speaking when people retire, there are two major expenditures they no longer have to deal with; one is the mortgage, the other is the children. So when you look at your lists you may be able to see that the difference between your salary and your pension is bridged by not having these two expensive items on your budget. Everyone realises that this does not mean you are never going to spend money on your children again, but it does mean that their running costs, and maintaining them in the manner to which they would like to become accustomed, is no longer your sole financial responsibility. In other words, the children can be put below the line, which means that they are amongst the items for which you can sort out your own priorities, according to the means at your disposal.

However, some people who retire early may still be paying for mortgage and children, in which case these outgoings will have to be above the line on your list, and careful juggling will be needed to continue with your usual standard of living. Some people in this situation will want to work, even part-time, to make up the financial difference; others will cut down on certain expenditures for the time being, knowing that it's a temporary measure. Having a list makes it much easier to work out what is needed. The important point to remember, though, is that the items above the line should be covered.

There are also some other decisions to be made. How should you invest your lump sums? Will you blow some of the money on that holiday of a lifetime? How should you arrange for your money to keep pace with inflation? If you sell your home for a smaller place, thus releasing some capital, where do you invest the balance? Do you go for income or growth? Should you buy an annuity? These are questions which confuse many people, at a time when you will be bombarded with offers and options through the letterbox and in the papers. After all, none of us are experts.

But Chris Ring is. He is a director of a City firm which has had 85 years' experience of acting for private investors, many of whom are people who are just retiring and want answers to some, if not all, of these questions. He has very positive views on the important criteria to consider when investing for those about to retire. He says:

> The most important priority in investing for retirement is, peace of mind – is your capital safe? Then the other priorities should be return, flexibility and tax efficiency, with a cash reserve for emergencies, and an element of growth in both income and capital as a protection against inflation.

That all seems very sound, but which types of investment do you choose? Chris Ring explains:

> There are six main types of investment – Deposits, Fixed Interest, Investments Linked to Equities, Personal Equity Plans (PEPs), Income Plans and Inflation-Proof Investments. The differing characteristics of each means that no one type will meet all needs. To meet the criteria in order of their importance to an individual, a mixture will often be needed to give the right balance. The investor will have to decide.

But how do you decide which is best for you? Chris ring again:

> Look at the lists you made and establish how much income you need. This will tell you how much return your capital must produce. Always remember to consider your tax

78

position, as this could affect the outcome of your decision. For instance, if your tax allowance is more than your income, then you would not be liable for tax at all. Up until now a building society investment would not have been best because the income is paid with tax already deducted and this cannot be reclaimed. In the future it can be. Building societies do give security and flexibility, depending on the type of account you have, so for those whose tax position is appropriate, this form of saving is very popular.

My advice on this form of investment is that deposits provide an excellent and convenient home for a cash reserve, but they have two possible shortcomings. The rate of interest can be varied from time to time, so for anyone relying on the interest as an important part of their income, a reduction in interest rates could be very damaging. The other drawback is that your capital doesn't grow, so while it is secure there is no prospect of capital appreciation.

Various methods of investment are examined below, and Chris Ring's comments are given at the end of each section.

Fixed Interest Investment

Fixed interest investments could be considered if you need to have a guaranteed level of income from your capital and you therefore want to protect yourself from falling interest rates. Or you may want security and to lock-in to what seem to be very high rates of interest; in this case you should consider investments offering a fixed and guaranteed return. Most of the investments in this category initially offer a return slightly lower than is available from deposits, reflecting the fact that it is fixed and cannot fail for the term of the investment, even if other interest rates are falling.

Most of the items available in this category are relatively very secure. But access, and therefore flexibility, varies considerably and must be carefully considered. These investments are especially suitable for those seeking a guaranteed level of income with low risk. There is, however, the risk that inflation will adversely affect the value of the investment overall. These investments are very attractive when rates of interest are high, but less attractive when they are low.

Investments Linked to Equities

While equities, or ordinary shares, offer good prospects for

79

maintaining the real value of income and capital in the long term, they normally provide a lower income than can be obtained elsewhere. You are, in fact, buying a share in the company and accordingly receive a proportion of the company's profit and growth in value. You can invest directly and own the shares outright, or invest indirectly through a managed fund such as unit trusts. Professional advice is recommended – and remember, shares can go down, and stay down for a long time, as well as go up.

It is unwise to put too large a proportion of your capital into this sort of investment. Indeed, anyone who is totally averse to risk should avoid them. As a guide, make sure that you have adequate cash for emergencies and that your income from other sources is secure. Do not be too dependent on the income from equities.

Personal Equity Plans (PEPs)

For anyone interested in shares or unit trusts, a personal equity plan (PEP) will provide a tax-efficient method of investing. Shares or unit trusts bought through a PEP have two distinct advantages; the dividend income is free of tax and, when the investments are sold, they are completely free of capital gains liability.

The government limits the amount that can be invested in a PEP annually. However, making use of the annual allowance, it will be possible over the years to build up a substantial portfolio which can provide a growing tax-free income. And if the value of the PEP rises significantly, it can then be sold without tax liability.

PEPs are equity-based and can provide good capital growth and an increasing income, thus offering a good hedge against inflation. But again, the value of shares can go down as well as up, so any money invested must not be needed for other purposes in the short term (say less than five years). However, because shares can rise or fall dramatically in value, many people are tempted to buy and sell them in the hope of realising extra profit. This is a strategy best left to experts.

Income and Growth Plans

These are special arrangements, offered by insurance companies, designed to provide a secure income, capital growth, or a mixture of the two. The plan usually consists of a combination of a temporary annuity at preferential rates, with an endowment policy. The annuity provides the flow of cash for the term of the plan to pay the annual endowment premiums, and to provide regular income. There are no medical requirements for the most common arrangements. Income plans generally run for ten years, although some five-year plans are available. Most of the companies offering these arrangements will allow an early surrender of the scheme, but the surrender value will not be guaranteed.

Choosing a good insurance company is more important than choosing the highest income or the best overall performance. There are other schemes where the annuity is replaced by investment bonds or gilts, with consequent effects on the security of the arrangement. Investment bonds are less secure because their value cannot be guaranteed in advance. Many people find that an income plan which provides a regular, guaranteed income, together with the prospect of a worthwhile tax-free capital sum when the plan matures after five or ten years, offers them an excellent base for their investments in retirement.

Inflation-Proof Investments
For the complete protection of capital against inflation, there are index-linked National Savings Certificates and index-linked British Government stocks (gilts).

These are useful for investors who like to feel that some part of their investment will maintain its real value, whatever happens to inflation. However, they suffer from the drawback that the income is low or non-existent.

TESSAs
There is also a new form of savings, available from January 1991, though the amount you can invest is limited. It is called TESSA – Tax Exempt Special Savings Account. This offers a tax-efficient way of saving if you can leave your money untouched for five years. It is an account with a bank or building society into which you can pay money, either on a regular basis, or as and when you have some to spare. According to the initial terms of the schemes, announced in the 1990 Budget, the total maximum amount permitted for saving is £9,000 (excluding interest) and if you prefer, you can make

lump sum payments, but no more than £3,000 in the first year, £1,800 in years two, three and four, and £600 in the fifth year.

If the money is left in for five years, the interest is tax-free. At the end of five years the account becomes taxable, but you can then close it and open a new one with part of the money – £3,000. You are allowed to have only one TESSA at a time.

It will be possible to draw out some of the interest if required during the five-year period, but it will then be taxed at source. However, that tax will be refunded to you at the end of the five years together with the total interest on the investment. If it becomes necessary to draw out any of the capital before the end of five years, you would have to close the TESSA and lose all the tax benefits you may have built up.

Banks and building societies will be able to decide on interest rates and other conditions so before you decide on which TESSA, compare what's on offer.

Conclusions

There are a number of other types of investment which may be useful in special circumstances, but the investments described above cover most needs. A person's tax position, the state benefits they are eligible for, their family responsibilities, whether or not they have a mortgage, and many other factors will determine which investment or mix of investments will suit them best financially and provide them with the peace of mind that is fundamental to good investment. Chris Ring concludes:

> As we have seen, there are many options and there are also many risks. One often reads about past performance of unit trusts and investment bonds, but this is no guarantee of what will happen in the future. And while on the subject of 'guarantees', make quite sure they apply to what you think they do. Items sometimes offer high guaranteed income, but what about the capital sum, which may not have any guarantee?

TAX

Tax is a specialist subject, which is presumably why there are so many tax advisers, tax accountants and tax lawyers, and no one should be criticised for feeling a fair amount of confusion in this area. For example, while the basic allowances you can claim are quite easy to understand, the application of the additional Age

Allowances for people over 65, and over 75, can be less clear, depending on the amount of earnings that may be involved if you continue working.

If your income (earnings and investment) is over the limit of the Age Allowance, currently (1990) £12,300 for those aged 65 to 74, it does mean that the Age Allowance will be scaled down progressively until it reaches the basic Personal Allowance. The important thing, therefore, is to make use of the separate taxation arrangements now available for husband and wife, if one or other spouse's income is low enough. These came into force in April 1990, and apply to all married couples regardless of age.

For instance, if a husband over 65 has a job in a higher tax bracket than his wife, and with other income, such as investments, he is receiving more than £12,300 per year, he can move investments which may be in his name to hers, thus attracting tax at the rate she pays, particularly if she is not paying any tax at all. If the wife is the higher earner the procedure can be reversed. One of the advantages of this development is the flexibility the new rules allow between husbands and wives. Of course, in such a situation you would have to be sure that the relationship is very secure, otherwise the question of attraction could involve more than tax; an unlucky husband could find his wife has spent his hard-earned money and, worse, has gone off not only with a toy-boy, but with his investments as well. Or, if the wife is the higher earner and transfers her investments to her husband, she should beware the bimbo!

Another aspect of the connection between decisions you need to make and your tax position could arise if you still have a mortgage to pay when you retire. Many people in this situation wonder whether they should use some of their lump sum retirement money to pay it off. But this depends on various factors, not least your tax position. For people in a high tax bracket, retaining the mortgage gives them tax relief at their higher rate of tax. For others, it may be better for some of the lump sum to be used to repay the mortgage, especially when interest rates are high, as this would help with your cashflow.

As you will see, tax can be very confusing, so you might find it helpful to get two booklets from the Inland Revenue which set out the various conditions and how they apply – IR 4, *Income Tax and Pensioners*, and IR 4a, *Income Tax/Age Allowance*. There is also a public enquiry office for the Inland Revenue.

Trying to match up the investments options already detailed to an individual's tax status can be an area where many would be glad of expert advice, but you may be wary about whether or not that advice would be impartial. Fortunately this need has been addressed through the Financial Services Act which came into being in 1987, ensuring that investment brokers and all those who were in a position of giving advice, i.e. accountants and banks, register with the Securities and Investments Board – a government watchdog – and that they elect whether or not they are 'tied'.

If they are 'tied', it means that the person giving advice represents a few particular companies, and therefore any advice they give you will be within the context only of what those companies have on offer. You could still be getting excellent advice, but it will be limited. A broker who is 'tied' is obliged legally to tell you so and, while the advice may be suitable for you, you have to know that it only encompasses the companies he or she represents. Then there are the general brokers who are not tied to any particular company, from whom you would obviously get a much wider choice of advice.

When you go to an adviser, the Financial Services Act requires that you sign a document stating that you understand you will be getting the best advice the adviser has to give and, most important for you, confirming that they are registered members of a professional institution with a code of conduct. Furthermore, any institutions the adviser belongs to must themselves comply with the regulations of the Securities and Investments Board.

FIMBRA, the Financial Intermediaries, Managers and Brokers Regulatory Association, is one of the institutions to which advisers must now belong. These institutions have the power to inspect books of member firms and to ensure separate clients' accounts are maintained. If any dishonesty occurs, they have the power to expel members, and they ensure that, to a certain extent, funds are protected, as with the Building Societies Association. However, the financial limit of protection may be very much smaller than your investment. It is wise to check the exact amount. Other institutions with similar powers are The Securities Assocation (TSA), the Investment Management Regulatory Organisation (IMRO) and Life Assurance and Unit Trust Regulatory Organisation (LAUTRO). Members of the public can also check whether a firm is authorised by consulting the SIB Central Register of Authorised Businesses, available on page 301 of Prestel or telephone 071-929 3652.

Since 1990 advisers have had to declare their commission earnings, which means that they will have to be seen to be fairly recommending different methods of investment, and the spread of commission they receive will reflect this procedure. It is this subject of commission that may have deterred people from seeking advice in the past. Advisers are quite entitled to charge for their time and expertise, particularly as what they have to say may save you money in the long run. However, professional advice does not usually come cheap and in order to avoid any misunderstandings you should check what their charges are. In some instances there is no charge, as their commission comes from the investments they are selling; in others, as in the case of solicitors and accountants, they usually charge on a time basis.

There's no need to be shy about approaching these specialists, even if you are not talking about a huge amount of money. You would be quite welcome with your lump sum, and other money you have to invest. This is how they earn their living. You are quite at liberty to seek advice from more than one adviser, but with each one you will be required to sign the letter mentioned above. On the whole, though, you will find that advisers tend to recommend a spread of investment if your resources allow it, giving you a combination of income and growth.

Capital Gains Tax

Not only will your income tax position have an important bearing on how you approach investments; capital gains tax and inheritance tax should also be considered.

The profit made when an asset is sold could be liable to capital gains tax, the most obvious exceptions being the profit on the sale of your main residence, your car and any fixed interest stocks. There is also an annual tax-free allowance, as well as other concessions.

Anyone who may be liable to this tax can minimise it by reviewing their investments before the end of the tax year and taking profits up to the tax-free limit. They can then, if they wish, re-purchase the same investments the next day; this is known as 'bed and breakfasting' – the cost of the commission on selling and buying back would normally be much less than the savings in capital gains tax.

Capital gains incurred above the annual allowance are added to your income and taxed as for income tax. Because the allowance exists, it makes sense in many cases to take advantage of it and this can only be done by investing in items which are likely to increase in value and are easily sold. Shares generally fit this description conveniently.

Inheritance Tax

This tax is payable when wealth is passed on and you are a beneficiary. The rules are complex, and often change, so it pays to be aware of the way the tax works and how to minimise its impact.

For a start, the lower the value of the estate, the lower will be the tax. But this is easier said than done, particularly if the major asset is the home, as is so often the case. Then there are circumstances where the seven-year rule may apply; in these cases it could mean that you can make over part or all of your assets, including your home, to your chosen beneficiary or beneficiaries and, if you do not die within seven years, they inherit without any liability for inheritance tax. This device may be of particular interest these days when property values have turned homes into major assets. However, the rules can vary, so advice must be sought.

WILLS

Regular reviews of your affairs, and ensuring your will is written, are both strongly recommended. It's not because you are no longer as young as you were that the subject of a will is raised; in fact many people make a will when they buy their first home. Despite that, seven out of ten people never make a will at all. So if you are one of them, now is the time to tidy up that loose end – loose ends have a nasty habit of tripping people up.

If you die without making a will, there's no problem if your house is jointly owned with your spouse (under a joint tenancy as it is known in legal terms) – it will go to the surviving spouse. But if it is jointly owned under a tenancy in common, that is in shares which may not be equal, then each party can dispose of their share as they wish; this means that if no will exists, the surviving spouse does not automatically inherit. And what many people don't realise is that, without a will, husbands or wives do not automatically inherit everything outright; they may have to share it with children, parents, or even more distant relatives, leaving them homeless and bereft.

The rules of inheritance, if a will does not exist, are laid down by statute, i.e. by law. If there are no blood relatives, the spouse gets everything. If there's a spouse and children, then what the spouse gets depends on the value of the estate. In some instances the spouse does not inherit everything, so without a will the wife, or husband, cannot be sure of getting the house. If no relatives at all are alive the Crown, i.e. the State, takes everything. In the case of a divorced or legally separated man or woman, that property does not go to the former spouse, though he or she may have other rights against the estate.

A more complicated situation arises with couples living together who are not recognised by law as being married. It is vital therefore that such couples should each make a will so that the remaining partner will be protected under the law; otherwise they could find themselves without a home or anything else.

Making a will is not complicated; in fact you can buy a form at a stationers and have it witnessed in accordance with the instructions on the form, although it should still be checked by a legal person to make sure it is valid. It is best therefore to go to a solicitor and have it drawn up professionally. The charges will not be excessive, and if you feel embarrassed about going to your regular solicitor if he or she should be a friend or connection, any solicitor will do this for you. Think it all out very carefully in advance so that when you go to have the document drawn up, you will be able to state clearly what you want as far as your partner, family, charities and any other intended beneficiaries are concerned.

You will need to appoint an executor. If your bank or a solicitor are to act in this capacity, check what their charges would be. After that, keep the will in your bank or another place of safe keeping, and tell your executor or a member of your family where it is.

Then, as long as you don't want to change it, you can forget all about it and get on with organising the best way in which to invest your leisure time so that it too will pay the highest dividends. It's best to be tidy, it will give you peace of mind – and as we've said, that's what it's all about.

6

WORK AND OTHER ACTIVITIES

'It's a demographic time bomb!' Mr Norman Fowler, the then Minister for Employment, said, launching a report in October 1989. He was referring to the declining pool of young people expected to come on to the labour market in the 1990s. But is this a new phenomenon? 'Employers who have a fixed retiring age for their employees should consider whether, in view of the present and prospective shortage of manpower, such a policy is in the national interest.' That comment was made by the social investigator Seebohm Rowntree in 1947.

In fact the figures confirm that the most dramatic changes have already taken place. Since 1973 the percentage of economically active males between 60 and 65 has fallen from 80 per cent to 50 per cent. By 1995 it is estimated that there will be 1.2 million fewer 16–24 year olds in the labour force than there were in 1987. But in a survey of 2,000 firms, while two-thirds of employers were aware of the problem, only one-third was trying to solve it.

Mr Fowler's pronouncement could well have been taken as a memo to employers that they should widen their recruitment horizons to include older workers, married women and 'returners', and should have a flexible approach to job sharing. That's all very well, many would say, but what do the employers think about it? Equally important, what do the older workers and others think about it, and do people really want to carry on working after retirement?

In truth, employers on the whole are somewhat resistant, though those companies known for their innovative overall approach are responding to the challenge. However, the general feeling is that there is still widespread discrimination against older people in the employment sector. Moreover, it is a fact that for a very long time the youth cult has dominated the employment market so that, in many instances, those in a position to recruit are themselves still very young; feelings of inhibition may well predominate at the suggestion that they should take on older people, who may in some cases be the same age as or older than their parents.

Age apart, a person's suitability for a job must also be considered; however liberal we may be in our approach, we have to be realistic. There are jobs for which some people are clearly unsuited, for a number of reasons, and one of these reasons may well be the stage of life the applicant has reached. This has traditionally been identified by 'years', but one person's capacity at a certain age may be higher or lower than that of another, so the yardstick of chronological age as a measure of suitability is not terribly reliable.

Yet blanket rules apply in most large organisations, so that people are retired by their companies at 55 or 60, sometimes even earlier, when a large number of them have many more years of active service to contribute. If they then wish to seek employment elsewhere, they are confronted with advertisements which to a large extent have tended to stipulate age barriers, whether 35 or 45. At the time of writing, amongst one day's quality paper's job advertisements, 31 per cent specified age.

Discrimination in whatever form is unacceptable, and no one is more passionate about this than Baroness Phillips, who introduced a Bill – Employment (Age Limits) – which was passed in the House of Lords in October 1989 at its Third Reading, but was too late for the Commons in that session. This Bill, if successful, would have made age discrimination illegal, as indeed it is in the United States. She feels legislation is the only way to redress the balance. She is supported by many interested organisations, including CAADE – the Campaign Against Age Discrimination in Employment. CAADE was formed by Philip Walker, whose own career came to an end in his late 40s; after hundreds of unsuccessful job applications, he discovered many other people in the same position and realised there was a need for legislation. CAADE has now joined forces with the Association of Retired Persons (ARP) who themselves are involved in a joint project – Age Works Over 50 – with ECCO a multinational employment group based in France.

But what about that 'demographic time bomb'? And in whose face is it going to explode? It could be the employers', if they refuse to receive the message the Minister was transmitting. Perhaps this is why there seems to be a mood of optimism creeping in as far as attitudes to older workers are concerned. As a matter of fact, the warning of that time bomb is sounding loud and clear, and a new trend seems to be emerging which some would say is discrimination of another kind. There is a growing realisation amongst some organisations that the older generation is a resource that should be wooed and courted, not only because there is a shortage of young workers, but for a more important reason – the older workers tend to have the very qualities that may be found lacking in the young. Some large food and DIY shops have advertised for people 'over 55' for junior and managerial positions. Tesco, for instance, have positively welcomed the 50–60 year olds and over; they say, 'They are more reliable, more conscientious and, unlike many young people, they have a natural instinct for customer service. They are the "customer is always right generation".'

So do we really need the legislation? Baroness Phillips is firm.

I know it may be said that the demographic curve means that the over-40s, and especially the over-50s are the best thing since sliced bread, and that suddenly they will return to the fold and everyone will want them. However, I think that the present situation shows not a real change of attitude on the part of the employer, but simply a change brought about by necessity. It only needs another swing for us to be back to square one, and for age to be used as a discriminatory factor again.

If the present situation does show a real change in theory, is this so in practice, and what are large employers doing to ensure that in future they are not going to be left with gaps in their workforce? At Marks & Spencer, where 1,200 people retire each year from a workforce of 60,000, they no longer specify age limits in their advertisements, but are actively making sure they get a substantial slice of the labour force cake in the future. Cherry Hughes, Assistant Manager of their Pensions Department, explains:

We have a special department set up to deal with this and are specifically developing bridges with schools, industry and universities, talking to the workers of the future, and telling them about retailing, which perhaps has not traditionally had a glamorous image.

At the the other end of the age scale, M & S are realistic about the need to retain their employees beyond their retirement age, which is 60 for management and 65 in stores (male and female in each case). She continues:

We think you're going to see more people in the 50–60 age groups carrying on in employment even though they are retired from their main career. If technology presents a problem, we will just have to give them more time to learn. Older people have more life experience and are more committed to achievement in their work because they are highly motivated. They are going to be a very active group even to 75.

Sainsbury's, who have 350 people retiring each year out of a workforce of 73,000, have a retirement age of 60 for management and 65 in their stores, but six months before a store's employee is due to retire, he or she can apply to stay on (at the moment this does not apply to management). Their job and health will then be reviewed, bearing in mind that health problems can increase in older people. Apart from reservations about the effect that continuing work after retirement age may have on pensions, Sainsbury's are very positive about employing older people; they believe they are more reliable, as they have already reared their families and so have less distractions. But only time will tell if this policy will apply to management level.

The story is very much the same at the Civil Service, where the retirement age is 60 for both men and women, though in their case the policy of retaining people beyond that age is not a global one. Each department has wide-ranging discretion to make use of part-time or current staff in the most effective way for their work requirements, and this could include job sharing or other alternative patterns of working. A spokesperson acknowledges that they have to be more flexible now in the light of the fast-changing work scene, and they have the matter constantly under review. They point out, however, that although the opportunity to stay on or return to work is being offered, many of their people don't want to do so if they have a good retirement package.

DO YOU WANT TO WORK?

The most important issue of all is how you yourself feel about working after retirement. For many, they can't wait to get away from work, put their feet up and relax. For others, financial considerations have to be taken into account; or they may find it a terrible wrench to give up work if their job is stimulating and exciting. At 60 or 65 you could well have as much as 20 active years ahead of you and, while you may not want to work for all of them, the prospect of continuing with your present job or starting another career could appeal.

So you find yourself at decision time. Of course, you will want to make it a joint decision with your partner; for instance, have they retired too, or have they a few years to go yet? If the latter, then you might not like the idea of being on your own all day, unless of course you have some particular hobby or occupation to pursue. Also, you will both need to discuss the financial side of the situation; your decision could be determined by a desire to maintain living standards you are not ready to give up. Finally, there is the question of the reality of looking for a job, answering advertisements, drawing up a CV (which you probably haven't done for many years), not to mention the interviews themselves, perhaps even facing disappointment if your applications are rejected. Do you want to put yourself in the firing line of this barrage? It could strike at your confidence, which may already be dented by having to leave your job at 50 or 55.

And if you decide to bite the bullet, there are yet more considerations to examine. Do you want paid work? Full- or part-time work? Would you want to stay in the same field, and at the same level if you had a choice? Or would you consider something different, and more junior? Then there's the business of commuting. As transport declines in efficiency and comfort, many people are glad to be able to give up what has now become an unwelcome chore, although, of course, if you have a chauffeur-driven limousine you certainly won't want to give that up.

Before we consider the options, it's as well also to examine your motivation if you are going to look for paid work. Is it the money, or the need to express your ability to contribute? For many people a drop in income when they leave a job can be quite dramatic and, depending on their pension arrangements, there may be a tremendous shortfall between what they used to earn and what they are now going to get, even with the addition of the state pension. However, this should in part be compensated by a reduction in expenses – hopefully the mortgage will be paid off, and there should be less expense, if any at all, with the children.

Just the same you might be happier having a bit more money than you think you are going to need. You will have budgeted for that rainy day, but what about the children's rainy day? Though they will be off your hands, and standing on their own two feet, they sometimes get their feet wet, expensively wet, and you will want to extend a helping hand. Another thing – grandchildren can be expensive too. Or you may want to be more adventurous with holidays, exploring further afield, and that all costs more too.

If you do want to work for financial reasons, then you must check what effect this may have on your tax position, especially if, in addition to your company pension, you are also getting a state pension. There is now no restriction on what you may earn as far as your state pension is concerned; however, you will still be required to pay tax at the current rate, so you will have to assess if it is worth it earning enough to push you into a higher tax bracket, and whether it's worth actually taking a state pension just yet.

If you can do without the state pension for a while, you can defer it for seven years (after which you must take it), which could reduce your tax liability and will enable you to have a bigger pension later, as it will be accumulating with interest. Do check also about national insurance contributions, which you should continue to pay if you retire early from work but have not yet reached retirement age. There is a useful leaflet IR 56/N139, *Employed or Self Employed*, available from any tax office which gives you further information in this area.

GOING OUT TO WORK

Having decided you want to continue going out to work, the next step is to decide between full-time and part-time work. Where do you start? For some people the idea of staying on with a company they have worked for for a number of years has many attractions. As we have shown, this possibility is increasing and brings with it the advantages of familiarity with the business and colleagues, and the relief of not having to go out and prove yourself all over again in the marketplace.

If you decide to try for work with another company within the same field, some of these advantages will still apply. You already know the scene, and your years of experience represent a valuable contribution. You are known in that business world, where you may have reached a respected level, and this will do wonders for your confidence. If you feel this is the right direction for you, make approaches to friends and contacts, preferably well before you leave your existing job. Nothing succeeds like success, and if you apply for a job when you are already in one, it gives you more confidence in your application, enabling you to project a more positive image at your interview, and can favourably affect the way in which a prospective employer reacts.

You may find you are offered a job which is junior to the one you had been doing. Don't refuse it out of hand, though it's understandable if that is your initial reaction. If you are still as active as ever and relish the prospect of working well beyond the conventional retirement age, it could be a disappointment and a blow to your confidence even to have to consider the prospect of taking a step down. This is where pre-retirement preparation could be so helpful, enabling you to view this new situation objectively, to see that this in fact could be constructive and is not a slur on your ability. Don't let your pride get in the way of thinking of the advantages. For example, a more junior position means less responsibility and less strain. You may hate the prospect of slowing the pace, but remember, too, we become very conditioned to stress, to the point where we feel we are going to miss it if it's not there. But once it's gone the disappointment becomes less sharp day by day, easier to live with; in time you feel better, look better, and everything else looks better too, without that band of tension distorting your view.

Some people are quite glad to give up the daily grind of commuting, feeling it would be nice for a change to get in the car and drive off for the day. But they don't want to give up work entirely, and want to continue earning. The answer for them is part-time work. This can give you the best of both worlds, as well as allowing you the opportunity to think about easing yourself into a position where you may give up work altogether.

Now that job sharing is becoming increasingly popular, the part-time field is broadening. Many agencies have part-time jobs available; and don't forget the Job Centres, which are used by firms looking for staff at all levels. Concentrate on agencies specialising in your particular skills – teaching, computer technology, executive and administration. If you belong to a trade association or a chamber of commerce, they could also be helpful. The local paper is another fruitful source.

Interesting part-time jobs are of course desirable, but this doesn't have to be such a priority now that you will have leisure time to spare for interesting pursuits. Ideally, something near home so that you can walk to work wouldn't be a bad thing either. You have got to get out of that car somehow.

Furthermore, paid work in the community is now being recognised as a worthwhile outlet for the skills and experience you may have gained in commerce or industry. These days, caring organisations have more need than ever of these skills. For example, charities are jockeying for position to get a larger slice of the financial cake, and much of that work has become, of necessity, competitive; each one needs to keep its name before the public, decision-makers and funding organisations. So if you have public relations skills and experience they could well be of enormous value and highly appreciated in such an organisation.

But you might wonder if you could cope with the culture shock, moving from a company with the cut and thrust of strictly commercial motivation to one at the opposite extreme, no matter how worthy the cause. Perhaps it would be nice to find out in advance. Employees of Marks & Spencer, BP, Ford and a few others may well have the opportunity to do just this, as part of one- or two-year secondment schemes these companies are operating, run under the auspices of the parent company for mid-career and pre-retirement employees. Sending these employees to non-profit-making organisations in the community benefits the company in terms of corporate image and staff morale, and brings corporate skills and objectivity to organisations which may need them but cannot afford them. Above all, for the secondee it could be a bridge to retirement which gives them an opportunity to examine and consider a different outlook and direction for the future. A one-day course called Action for Change is run by the Industrial Society in conjunction with the Action Resource Centre; it takes place twice a year in London and offers practical advice on how to make the most of this kind of secondment and of a wide variety of work in the voluntary sector.

APPLYING FOR A JOB

It's important to spend some time assessing all the different options carefully and well in advance. But eventually you will have to prepare a CV. CV is short for *curriculum vitae*, and it should list all the stages of your working life. It will probably have been many years since you completed a CV, so the prospect could be daunting.

For those who can afford it, the private recruitment consultancies will help you in this direction; they may even try to place you in a job. Their fees will probably be quite high, but you may feel it's worth it.

But if your CV is to be a DIY exercise there's no need to panic. Where do you start? First make a list of your qualifications and training. Next come the jobs you have had, with the dates, names and details of companies you worked for, what their business was, what your duties were, and possibly the salary you earned in each case. What prospective employers will be looking for will be a record which shows progress in position and experience, with preferably not too many moves, or gaps. If there are gaps, explain them.

The CV should be well spaced out and no more than two or three pages, depending on the job you are applying for. Your name, address and daytime telephone number should go at the head of the first page, and the names and addresses of two or three referees at the end. Give only relevant information, and type it out unless specified otherwise. If you can't manage the typing, there are typing agencies that will do this for you, laying out the CV professionally, and they are not expensive.

When applying for a job a short covering letter along with the CV is a good idea, just stating clearly why you are applying for the job, why you feel you could contribute to the work of the company, and just a sentence or two on what you believe your advantages are over a younger person.

Do study advertisements very carefully before you apply. Make sure they really are suitable for you and you for them. Don't apply immediately you see an ad; wait for the next day and read it over again. You won't have lost any time but you may well have gained an objectivity with which to view it and you could well find it is not for you after all. This would have saved you the trouble of applying and the disappointment of rejection.

If you have managed the CV, how about the interview itself?

Whether you know the company or not, it can be an ordeal. Do some homework beforehand so that you can demonstrate that you have a knowledge of and interest in their products or activities. A look at their annual report will give you an overall picture. Have an answer prepared if they should ask you why you think they should choose you over the other applicants – remember, all the applicants are likely to be asked this question. If you are faced with an interview board, be prepared to field questions which could undermine your confidence, such as, 'Do you think at your age you could cope with the pressure, etc.?' Talk objectively about previous companies you have worked for without being derogatory, even if you feel like that. Above all, be quietly confident – you still have a lot to contribute.

CAREER COUNSELLING AND JOB REGISTERS

If you get a job, fine. But if you don't you may feel your age is the problem. You may be right, so you could hardly be blamed for asking, 'What's all this I keep hearing about how desirable it is to have older people, and how it's so necessary to make up the reduction of young people, yet I can't get a job. What's going on?' The process of change takes time, not only for employers, but for you too. Maybe you are aiming in the wrong direction.

For those to whom it is important to continue working but who find themselves unable to get a job, career counselling, if you can afford it, has become very popular. Assessment interviews can start at £250 and may cost even more in the end. They won't even find you a job, but their value lies in helping you to re-assess yourself and your abilities, and point you in directions you may not have thought of, to which you may be more suited and which may be more appropriate to you. The best thing to do if you are contemplating going to one of these organisations is to get a selection of their brochures and study them to see whether they have on offer what you want. You could check with the career counsellor of your company before you leave to see if they could recommend one firm or another in this field.

More reasonable fees are charged by the National Advisory Centre on Careers for Women. This is a registered charity, noncommercial, and the cost for an interview with information and perhaps even some training should be around £50 (see Useful addresses on page 122). (Their Executive, Kalyani Menon, has written a helpful book *Returners in the '90s* (Cassell, spring 1991.)

There are also some government services which may be helpful, and for which you will not need to pay a fee. Job Centres are a good place to start. The staff there will be able to tell you about retraining opportunities; the Restart Programme, for instance, is a one-week course covering such subjects as drawing up a CV, and interview technique. From there you might go to a Jobclub; these are self-help groups where you can have free use of typing, photocopying and, again, tips on interview technique.

Retraining opportunities are detailed in an informative book, *Second Chances*, which is available from the Training Commission (see Useful addresses on page 122). At the time of writing the price is £9.95, but it may be available in your public library. Women who have stopped work to raise a family, or anyone who has been away from the workforce for a period of time, could find all these services helpful. 'Returners', as these people are sometimes called, very often still have the skills, but they may be rusty, which in turn can lead to a lack of confidence when looking for a job.

The Professional and Executive Register is a free service which will try to match those looking for work with companies looking for employees. There are 23 branches nationally and details may be found in your local Yellow Pages. *Executive Post* is another useful way of finding out what vacancies there are; on payment of £5 you are sent a copy every Wednesday for 13 weeks, and can continue for longer if you wish.

Other prospects may only be for a minority, but are worth mentioning as they could spark off other ideas for you. The Emeritus Network is a non-profit-making organisation for members over 50 who seek new careers and opportunities in full-time or part-time work, or business ventures (see Useful addresses on page 121). The annual subscription is £25, and they will give guidance on planning workshops which help transition from a main career to a new one, and try to place you from their comprehensive database of information on vacancies.

The prospect of being a non-executive director may sound ideal, with its combination of some work, using all the experience you have, and some leisure, with no loss of pride. Needless to say it is very difficult to find these directorships, but you could try applying to Promotion of Non-Executive Directors (PRONE) for details – they maintain a register of applicants in different size companies, but in order to qualify for their register you will need to have served on the board of a public limited company. Another place to contact is the Institute of Directors, Board Appointments and Consultancy Service – membership of the IOD is not necessary (see Useful addresses on page 121).

Then there is the Temporary Executive Service launched by the CBI. This might enable you to find appointments in a specialist field for a short term, say a few months or possibly even longer. You will find details at the Executive Service, Manpower Department, CBI (see Useful addresses on page 121). There is also an office in Scotland.

There is also the agency Success After Sixty. Despite their name they consider people from 50 upwards, specialising in secretarial staff, book-keepers and people with computer skills. They generally only place people in central London, though (see Useful addresses on page 122).

If you are inclined towards the unusual and want part-time work, you could try working as a courier for Carefree Camping in France. This is a company which specialises in family camping holidays (see Useful addresses on page 121). In 1974 they asked an older couple who were friends of the director to help out. It was a roaring success, and they have been employing older couples ever since. They recruit about 70 couples each summer for four months, but you need to have stamina – the work can be hard, preparing the accommodation, welcoming families when they arrive and being on hand with advice and practical assistance whenever needed. You will need to know a foreign language; perhaps you will have worked in education. Such mature couples are extremely popular with the families and the parents; the managing director Mark Hammerton says, 'We find older couriers are very responsible and dependable; they are better at socialising with our clients, they are better in a crisis and they don't treat the job as a working holiday.'

While still in the holiday department, if you are interested in your heritage and are very energetic and extrovert, then you could think about becoming a tour guide. You would have to do a course which is run by the British Travel Association, and in London it would be necessary to pass the London Tourist Exam. The work would obviously be seasonal and you would get paid by the day. But this could bring out the theatrical side of you as you lead tourists over a stately home telling them how heads rolled, backs were stabbed, and showing them beds where famous people of the past are supposed to have slept while dark plots were hatched.

CONSULTANCY WORK

For those with particular skills, acting as a consultant could be quite interesting and lucrative. In some cases it may even be possible to do consultancy work for the company you are leaving; as far as they are concerned, they can then save on your overheads while retaining your expertise, having trained you maybe, while for you it is an ideal way of maintaining contact with colleagues and fulfilling the need for a professional role when you retire. The beauty of consultancy work is of course that, as a free agent, you are in a position to accept work from other contacts you have made during your career and to whom your expertise has been proven. In particular, consultancy work may be a service which is more attractive to smaller companies or companies who are just starting up in business and who do not want to take on the overheads of full-time staff. Or it may be possible to get your name on the list of a few larger consultancies that have registers they call on when particular skills are involved. There is also a register published by the Institute of Management Consultants; it may be necessary for you to join, so check with them. They also publish booklets on the subject.

There are many areas where consultancy may be possible, far too numerous to list. Just ask yourself if the work you are qualified for, and have been doing, could be of use on an *ad hoc* basis. Broadly speaking anyone with a particular expertise in areas connected with public relations, marketing or economics are in demand. Computer technology is also a growth area. You may have to invest in equipment, though if you have a regular contract with a particular company they may be prepared to supply it for you to use at home.

Professionals in other areas too can become consultants. For instance, someone who has worked in the commercial property section of a legal office will have contacts among building developers. There is then a chance of being retained as an adviser for potential transactions. Again previous contacts would be well worth approaching just to inform them that you are available and what areas of expertise you have to offer as far as their particular business is concerned.

The Institute of Directors have a board appointments consultancy service and it would be well worth while contacting them for advice on the subject of part-time consultancy work (see Useful addresses on page 121).

The Department of Employment have a Small Firms Service which operates in different parts of the country, with a team of counsellors to advise and assist people starting out in business. While this would cover quite a wide selection, it could well be that your expertise and business experience would qualify you to be one of their counsellors. There is a centre in each region which you can contact through Freephone Enterprise.

Information technology is another area, and here disabled people too can help to fill a growing need for personnel, often working from home. The Department of Employment have a disabled advisory service which provides training, recruitment and, in some cases, grants for equipment. However, many disabled people are not aware of the opportunities, but the British Computer Society, through their Specialist Group for the Disabled, are seeking to raise awareness amongst employers and the disabled alike.

RUNNING A BUSINESS FROM HOME

More than one million people in the United Kingdom run businesses from their homes. Home businesses may not always turn you into a millionaire, though there are exceptions, but there are many advantages.

If you and your partner have particular skills to contribute, you could find great satisfaction in sharing your hours together in a constructive way to add to your income. Women who have never gone out to work, or perhaps who have only worked part-time, need not feel at a disadvantage. Indeed, women are excellent organisers, running a home providing some of the best experience any administrator could get.

If you have never been involved in the responsibility of running a business before, it's very important to get professional help and advice about setting it up in order to see exactly what you may be letting yourself in for. A phone call to Free-phone Enterprise, who run a Small Firms Service, will bring starter packs giving helpful information covering the possibility of grants and contact points if you want to take the matter further.

When starting a business you may be faced with some expenses and overheads, and you may find that this is not money that you will earn back in the first year, or even longer, so be prepared. Before going ahead, put a plan on paper – the Enterprise pack will show you how – and get advice from an accountant, solicitor or bank manager, or someone who is familiar with your abilities and financial resources.

The other thing to remember is that working from home means you are limiting the possibility of leisure time. Somehow working at home, without the structure and routine of someone else's business, you tend to work tremendously long hours, feeling perhaps this is necessary in order to become established. So think carefully, or you may find yourself working harder than you did before, with all the added responsibility that your own business entails.

If you decide to go ahead you must go into the question of tax very thoroughly. Two booklets issued by the Inland Revenue, IR 28 and IR 57, are essential reading. There are pros and cons. One of the pros is that if you are using a part of your home exclusively for business, you are very likely to get a tax allowance on a portion of your heating, light, rates, in-surance and telephone; if you are still paying a mortgage, it may be possible that this would be included too. But the dis-advantage is that if you sell your home, you may be liable for capital gains tax on the proportion of space you use solely for business. If the room you use for work doubles as a TV room, guest room or similar, and is not exclusively for business, then it is likely you would not be charged capital gains tax, but there is no guaranteed rule about this. A booklet, CGT 4, is available from your local tax office giving you details of what may be allowable. You must get the financial situation clearly defined well in advance.

The cons also need to be very carefully considered. If you are operating as a sole trader, you are liable for all the debts of your business if it is not a success, and this extends to your personal assets, not just those of the business. This means that if things get so bad that you are made bankrupt, you may find yourself forced to sell your home in order to pay your creditors. So be sure that any money you put into your business is money you can afford to lose if the worst comes to the worst and you are caught in a downturn. Also, get advice from a solicitor if there is a possibility that you would want to use your home as a guarantee for a loan; this arrangement is not one that should be entered into lightly.

There could also be pitfalls involved in raising finance, such as high interest rates, which can play havoc with your cashflow. You will therefore need to be on more than nodding terms with accounts (whether on paper or computerised), VAT and tax returns, and with contracts of employment if you will have people working for you.

If your home is not owned freehold, the terms of your lease or tenancy agreement will need to be checked by a solicitor. Generally speaking if your home is just used as an office there would probably be no problem, but if your business involves many callers, it could raise problems with your lease and with neighbours too. It could also mean that your poll tax would be converted to business rates. Furthermore, there is always the possibility that planning permission and higher insurance could be involved. Even with a freehold property, these matters should be taken into consideration.

Another thing to think about is what to do if you have a long period of illness. If there's just you and your partner, or just you yourself, it can mean non-delivery of your products, which means money isn't coming in. Some insurance companies now offer policies which pay out not only on death, but also on protracted illness. This may be worth looking into.

But if you still think this is for you, there is the question of choosing which business you would like to start. The best advice is to be involved in something of which you have considerable experience, perhaps connected to your previous work. This has the added advantage of contacts, who could turn into possible clients or customers.

Alternatively, choose something which is familiar to you as a hobby and which you know is marketable. For instance there are some DIY enthusiasts who produce custom-built chairs, tables and other items of furniture for discerning clients. The work is very high quality, much of it done by hand, with thorough attention to detail. Each piece is really a labour of love. This sort of endeavour may not be a big earner, but it could be very fulfilling. Probably your local paper would be interested in doing a feature if you needed publicity.

Talents in the field of arts and crafts could also be turned into a successful business if you are skilled in a particular way. One woman whose hobby was restoring dolls' houses is now an accepted authority on the subject, contributing articles internationally, and at retirement age is the author of a definitive book on the subject. Whatever you choose to do, though, assess the market to ensure that there will be a demand for your product or service, and that producing it will not involve you in more expense than you can comfortably bear.

Running a business from home could be tremendously satisfying, but it could also be a minefield set in what looks like a beautiful expanse of green meadow. You will be charting a very new path and, as with all journeys of this kind, you must equip yourself with a mine detector, and a water diviner so that if your supply of water runs out you won't die of thirst. Be sure to prepare yourself beforehand with all the facts, figures and necessary formalities which may be required of you. While it's a potentially exciting experience, it is to be approached with great caution and after a lot of discussion with your partner and your advisers. Out of that one million people who start their own businesses every year, sadly, many of them fall by the wayside.

CREATIVE WORK

But you don't have to go into business to get a productive kick out of those later years. If you are creative, a writer for instance, now is your chance to write the great novel or the definitive biography – it's never too late to start. The well-known novelist Mary Wesley had her first novel published at the age of 70. The famous American artist Grandma Moses started painting when she was a granny. And a composer called Minna Keel, aged 80, had a symphony of hers receive its premiere at the Proms in London in September 1989, to critical acclaim. When she was a young student at the Royal Academy of Music she dreamed of becoming a composer, but her life went in a completely different direction. The spark stayed alive though, and burst into flame when she retired and started composing at the age of 66.

When I retired I really felt as if I was running down and thought it was the evening of my life, but since I started composing I feel 20 years younger. I have always been

104

struggling to do something with my life and I try to express all that in my music. Instead of feeling that my life is behind me, it's all in front. All the dreams I had when I was studying are coming true. I feel like a teenager!

Well, we may not all be able to write a bestseller, be a famous painter or have a symphony performed at the Proms, but the important thing is to believe that it's never too late to try and to understand that, by trying, we are contributing, and so enriching our lives.

VOLUNTARY WORK

During a person's working life they rarely think of voluntary work. This is understandable. In a busy life there's no time for anything else. Voluntary work is something you may have thought of as 'for other people'. But when you stop work the sense of commitment you had for the job can be transferred in a less intense and less time consuming way to voluntary work, if you now have the inclination.

There are an estimated 27 million volunteers in the UK, with a greater need for them than ever. Numbers have been falling, caused in part by demographic changes – there are fewer young people to volunteer, while at the same time there has been an increase in the number of older people needing their help. Dr Justin Davis Smith, research officer of the Volunteers Centre UK, believes another cause is the decline in the number of middle-class women who have traditionally made up the majority of the volunteer force, as they are now being attracted back into paid employment.

Instead, far more men are now becoming involved, and it is hoped that whatever shortfall there is will be made up by people over 65 and persons from ethnic communities. Interestingly enough, it is the 16–24 year olds who do a large amount of the voluntary work for the sick and elderly.

Everyone is qualified to do voluntary work, whether they are professional, executive, running a home and family, doing office work, working in a shop, whatever, and if you prefer to offer any of these particular skills you will find many outlets. Or you might feel happier about becoming involved in a more general way, through your church or local hospital or community centre. The important thing is to make a commitment, and not to take on any more than you think you can cope with. A few hours a week, every week, is better than spasmodic bursts which can disrupt the organiser and the people you are trying to help.

It's also important to establish exactly what is expected of you, whether any expenses are paid, or if there are free meal vouchers. You may find yourself sharing a task with another volunteer; getting on with each other is important, even if you have to try a little – they may be trying too.

It's important, too, to decide which area of work would suit you best. The list is long, but basically the choice includes getting involved with children and young people, the elderly, the handicapped, the mentally ill, families, and many others. Maybe you want contact with the public, or perhaps you would prefer to be behind the scenes helping to provide a support system without which the organisation couldn't exist. Sometimes the work involves people who are needy in a way you never thought of; for instance, there is a scheme to assist children who need help and encouragement with their reading. Or there are Friends of the Earth, who need help with administration and other tasks. Or you could work on the telephone lines which now exist as a verbal haven for people who are troubled; the Samaritans provide a lifeline for their many callers, as does Childline. Training is usually given, as it is by the Citizens' Advice Bureaux for the volunteers who give advice in their offices.

The *Directory of National Voluntary Bureaux* gives a comprehensive list of needy categories, and many towns now have their own volunteer offices which will help you find work in specific areas. REACH, the Retired Executive Clearing House, can put executives in touch with community projects which need their top level skills and experience but can't afford them (see Useful addresses on page 122).

RSVP, the Retired and Senior Volunteer Programme, is an innovative concept. It offers retired people over 50 the opportunity to participate in a number of projects for the benefit of the local community. These volunteers work in groups, and anyone in the group can suggest a new project – perhaps helping at the local hospital, manning tourist information kiosks, or assisting at an art gallery.

If it is difficult to get out, you can still help, for example arranging coffee mornings which contribute to fund raising – many charities will help you to think up ideas. Or perhaps there's a young neighbour who would be very grateful for a break if you could take their youngster for a few hours.

The Red Cross is the world's largest humanitarian organisation, and needs a wide variety of volunteers, from beauty care and welfare duties to administrative and management skills. Or if you are prepared to travel abroad, the British Executive Service Overseas is a scheme to help developing countries create business organisations in their countries. Assignments are short-term, three to four months, and they need people with managerial, technical and professional skills. No salary is paid but partners are allowed to go too, and all travel, accommodation, subsidy and incidental expenses are paid.

And to let the animals have the last bark, if you would like to share the pleasure your dog can give, there is an organisation called PRO Dogs (see Useful addresses on page 122). This is a national charity which arranges visits to hospices, old people's homes and children's hospitals where the patients or residents can enjoy the warmth and affection that a friendly animal gives and inspires. A scientific survey conducted by the Companion Animal Research Group at Cambridge University found that, in the words of Dr James Serpell who was in charge, 'Pet keeping has a positive impact on people's physical and mental well-being.' No doubt the dogs won't object to all that extra attention.

CONCLUSION

It is often said that each age has its compensations. It may not always seem so for some people. But the one thing everyone will have on reaching the Third Age is experience of life. It will have taught you that time is precious, so you must use it in the best possible way for yourself and for others, whatever your circumstances. That's all very well, you may say, but if you feel a nasty twinge when you stretch your arm up to reach for the moon, let alone jump over it, or if you feel that life doesn't have a great deal to offer, what then? Try to go on believing that there's always something, and think of what Saul Bellow, the 75-year-old American author has to say, 'I am a true adorer of life, and if I can't reach as high as the face of it, I plant my kiss somewhere lower down.'

USEFUL ADDRESSES

GENERAL

UK

Age Concern (England)
60 Pitcairn Road
Mitcham
Surrey CR4 3LL
Tel: 081-640 5431

Age Concern (Northern Ireland)
128 Great Victoria Street
Belfast BT2 7BG
Tel: 0232 45729

Age Concern (Scotland)
33 Castle Street
Edinburgh EH2 3DN
Tel: 031-225 5000/1

Age Concern (Wales)
1 Park Grove
Cardiff CF1 3BJ
Tel: 0222 371566

Centre for Policy on Ageing
25/31 Ironmonger Row
London EC1V 3QP
Tel: 071-253 1787

Help the Aged
16/18 St James' Walk
London EC1R 0BE
Tel: 071-253 0253

The Pre-Retirement Association of Great Britain and Northern Ireland
Department of Educational Studies
Nodus Building
University of Surrey
Guildford GU2 5XM
Tel: 0483 393905

Includes a resource centre.

EIRE

Foundation of Active Retirement Associations
Ardenga Park
Blackrock
County Dublin
Tel: 01 802615

National Council for the Aged
Corrigan House
Fenian Street
Dublin 2
Tel: 01 766484

The Retirement Planning Council
16 Harcourt Street
Dublin 2
Tel: 01 783600

CHAPTER 2: HEALTH

UK

Alzheimer's Disease Society
158–160 Balham High Road
London SW12 9BN
Tel: 081-675 6557

Arthritis and Rheumatism Council (ARC)
41 Eagle Street
London WC1R 4AR
Tel: 071-405 8572

Back Pain Association
31–33 Park Road
Middlesex TW11 0AB
Tel: 081-977 5474

British Association of Cancer United Patients (BACUP)
121–123 Charterhouse Street
London EC1M 6AA
Tel: 071-608 1661,
or from outside London Freephone 0800 181199

*Telephone and letter advice and support service by qualified
nurses for patients, families and friends*

British Heart Foundation
102 Gloucester Place
London W1H 4DH
Tel: 071-935 0185

Disabled Living Foundation
380–384 Harrow Road, London W9 2HU
Tel: 071-289 6111

Family Heart Association
9 West Way
Botley
Oxford OX2 0JB
Tel: 0865 798969

Health Education Authority
Hamilton House
Mabledon Place
London WC1A 9TX
Tel: 071-383 3833

Inland Revenue Public Enquiry Room
West Wing
Somerset House
Strand
London WC2R 1LB
Tel: 071-438 6420/6425

Institute of Complementary Medicine
21 Portland Place
London W1N 3AF
Tel: 071-636 9543

The Keep Fit Association
16 Upper Woburn Place
London WC1H 0QG
Tel: 071-387 4349

The National Osteoporosis Society
PO Box 10
Barton Meade House
Radstock
Bath BA3 3YB

Relaxation for Living
29 Burwood Park Road
Walton-on-Thames
Surrey KT12 5LH

Weight Watchers
1 Thames Street
Windsor SL4 1SW
Tel: 0753 56751

**Women's Health and Reproduction Rights Information
 Centre**
52/54 Featherstone Street
London EC1Y 8RT
Tel: 071-251 6580

EIRE

Arthritis Foundation of Ireland
1 Sydney Parade Avenue
Dublin 4
Tel: 01 691737

Health Promotion Unit
Department of Health
Hawkins House
Hawkins Street
Dublin 2

Irish Cancer Society
5 Northumberland Road
Dublin 4
Tel: 01 681855

Irish Heart Foundation
4 Clyde Road
Dublin 4
Tel: 01 685010

CHAPTER 3: RELAXATION AND LEISURE

UK

Association of Railway Preservation Societies
3 Orchard Close
Watford
Hertfordshire WD1 3DU

British Gliding Association
Tel: 0533 531051

Central Council of Physical Recreation
Friends House
Francis Street
London SW1P 1DE
Tel: 071-828 3163

Council for the Accreditation of Correspondence Colleges
27 Marylebone Road
London NW1 5JS
Tel: 071-935 5391

Department of Trade and Industry (DTI)
10/18 Victoria Street
London SW1H 0NN
Tel: 071-215 5000

The English Tourist Board
Thames House
Blacks Road
London W6 9EZ
Tel: 081-846 9000

Independent Association of Time-share Owners
11/13 Waterloo Place
Leamington Spa
Warwickshire CV32 5LB
Tel: 0926 450843

MASTA
London School of Tropical Medicine
Keppel Street
London WC1E 7HT
Tel: 071-631 4408

National Gardens Scheme
57 Lower Belgrave Street
London SW1W 0LR

The Northern Ireland Tourist Board
River House
48 High Street
Belfast BT1 2DS
Tel: 0232 231221/7

The Open University
Walton Hall
Milton Keynes
Buckinghamshire MK7 6AA

Polytechnic Central Administration System
PO Box 67
Cheltenham
Gloucestershire GL50 3AP

The Pre-Retirement Association *see under general addresses*
  above

SEAVETS
34 Nash Grove Lane
Wokingham
Berkshire RG11 4HD
Tel: 0734 743634

The Scottish Tourist Board
23 Ravelston Terrace
Edinburgh EH4 3EU
Tel: 031-332 2433

The Sports Council
16 Upper Woburn Place
London WC1H 0QP
Tel: 071-388 1277

Time to Learn (NIACE)
19b De Montfort Street
Leicester LE1 7GE

Travel Companions
63 Mill Lane
London NW6 1NB
Tel: 071-431 1984 or 081-202 8478
(helps those who are looking for company to share a holiday)

Universities' Central Council on Admission (UCCA)
PO Box 28
Cheltenham
Gloucestershire GL50 1HY

University of the Third Age
6 Parkside Gardens
London SW19 5EY
Tel: 071-833 4747

The Welsh Tourist Board
Brunel House
2 Fitzalan Road
Cardiff CF2 1UY
Tel: 0222 499909

EIRE

Board Failte
Baggot Street Bridge
Dublin 2
Tel: 01 765871

Rail Europ, CIE
35 Lower Abbey Street
Dublin 1
Tel: 01 300777

CHAPTER 4: RELATIONSHIPS

UK

Age Concern *see under general addresses above*

The Association to Aid the Sexual and Personal Relationships of People with Disabilities (SPOD)
286 Camden Road
London N7 0BJ
Tel: 071-607 8851

The British Association for Counselling
37a Sheep Street
Rugby
Warwickshire CV21 3BX
Tel: 0788 78328/9

British Federation of Care Home Proprietors
51 Leopold Road
Felixstowe
Suffolk IP11 7NR
Tel: 0394 279539

Carers' National Association
29 Chilworth Mews
London W2 3RG
Tel: 071-724 7776

Children Need Grandparents
2 Surrey Way
Laindon West
Basildon
Essex
Tel: 0268 414607

Counsel and Care for the Elderly
131 Middlesex Street
London E1 7JF
Tel: 071-247 9844

CRUSE
Cruse House
126 Sheen Road
Richmond
Surrey TW9 1UR
Tel: 081-940 4818

The Divorce Conciliation Advisory Service
38 Ebury Street
London SW1W 0LU
Tel: 071-730 2422

Help the Aged *see under general addresses above*

National Association of Grandparents
8 Kirkley Drive
Ashington
Northumbria NE63 9RD
Tel: 0670 817036

**National Confederation of Registered Residential Care
  Homes Associations**
8 Southampton Place
London WC1A 2EF
Tel: 071-405 2277

Registered Nursing Homes Association
75 Portland Place
London W1N 4AN
Tel: 071-631 1524

Relate (formerly the Marriage Guidance Council)
Little Church Street
Rugby
Warwicks CV21 3AP
Tel: 0788 73241

EIRE

Bereavement Counselling Service
St Anne's
Dawson Street
Dublin 2
Tel: 01 767127

The Retirement Planning Council *see p. 110*

CHAPTER 5: HOME AND FINANCE

Age Concern *see under general addresses above*

Anchor Housing Association
Oxenford House
13/15 Magdalen Street
Oxford OX1 3BP
Tel: 0865 72226

Association of British Insurers
Aldermay House
10–15 Queen Street
London EC4N 1TT
Tel: 071-248 4477

British Federation of Care Home Proprietors *see page 116*

Building Employers' Federation
BEC Headquarters
82 New Cavendish Street
London W1
Tel: 071-580 5588

Department of Social Security (DSS) England
Alexander Fleming House
London SE1 6BY
Tel: 071-407 5522. State benefits free phoneline 0800 666555

DSS Northern Ireland
Dundonald House
Upper Newtownards Road
Belfast BT4 3ST
Tel: 0232 650111. State benefits free phoneline 0800 616757

DSS Scotland
3 Lady Lawson Street
Edinburgh EH3 9SH
Tel: 031-229 9191. State benefits free phoneline 0800 666555

DSS Wales
Government Buildings
St Agnes Road
Gabalfu
Cardiff CF4 4YJ
Tel: 0222 693131. State benefits free phoneline 0800 666555

Department of Social Security
Overseas Branch
Newcastle-upon-Tyne NE98 1YX

Good Housekeeping
PO Box 325
London SW4 9JZ

Help the Aged *see under general addresses above*

Inland Revenue Public Enquiry Office *see page 111*

Learning Materials Service Office
Open University
PO Box 188
Milton Keynes MK7 6DH

**National Confederation of Registered Residential Care
Homes Associations** *see page 116*

The National Supervisory Council for Intruder Alarms
Queensgate House
14 Cookham Road
Maidenhead
Berkshire SL6 8AJ
Tel: 0628 37512

New Homes Marketing Board
82 Cavendish Street
London W1M 6AD

Paddington Church Housing Association (PCHA)
Care and Repair
1-2 Drake's Courtyard
291 Kilburn High Road
London NW6 7JR
Tel: 071-372 3269

Park Housing Association Scheme
Brett House
Park Road
London W10 4HT
Tel: 081-961 2277

Securities and Investment Board Central Register of Authorised Businesses
3 Royal Exchange Buildings
London EC3V 3NL
Tel: 071-283 2474

EIRE

The Department of Social Welfare
Information Section
Store Street
Dublin 1
Tel: 01 786466

Financial Information Service Centre (FISC)
87–89 Pembroke Road
Dublin 4
Tel: 01 680400

Irish Security Industry Association
463 Collins Avenue
Dublin 9
Tel: 01 374918

CHAPTER 6: WORK AND OTHER ACTIVITIES

British Executive Service Overseas
10 Belgrave Square
London SW1X 8PH
Tel: 071-235 0991

CAADE (Campaign Against Age Discrimination in Employment)
395 Barlow Road
Altrincham
Cheshire WA14 5HW

Carefree Camping
126 Hempstead Road
King's Langley
Hertfordshire
Tel: 0923 261311

Emeritus Network
1st Floor
Quadrant Arcade Chambers
Romford RM1 3EH
Tel: 0708 46441/2

Executive Post
Rex House
4 Lower Regent Street
London SW1Y 4PP
Tel: 071-930 3484

The Executive Service
Manpower Department
CBI
Centrepoint
New Oxford Street
London WC1A 1DU
Tel: 071-379 7400

Institute of Directors
Board Appointments and Consultancy Service
116 Pall Mall
London SW1Y 5ED
Tel: 071-839 1233

Institute of Management Consultants
5th Floor
32/33 Hatton Garden
London EC1N 8DL
Tel: 071-242 1803/2140

National Advisory Centre on Careers for Women
4th Floor
2 Valentine Place
London SE1 8QH
Tel: 071-401 2280

National Association of Volunteer Bureaux
St Peter's College
College Road
Saltley
Birmingham B8 3TE
Tel: 021-327 0265

PRO Dogs
Rocky Bank
4 New Road
Ditton
Maidstone
Kent ME20 6AD
Tel: 0732 848499

Promotion of Non-Executive Directors
1 Kingsway
London WC2B 6XF
Tel: 071-240 8305

Retired Executive Clearing House (REACH)
89 Southwark Street
London SE1
Tel: 071-928 0452

RSVP, Community Service Volunteers
237 Pentonville Road
London N1 9NJ
Tel: 071-278 6601

Success After Sixty
40/41 Old Bond Street
London W1X 3AF
Tel: 071-629 0672

The Training Agency
Moorfoot
Sheffield S14
Tel: 0742 753275
Formerly the Manpower Services Commission

The Training Commission
Department CW
ISCO 5
The Paddock
Frising Hall
Bradford BD9 4HD

MAGAZINES

UK

Choice (monthly)
Choice Publications Ltd
3rd Floor
2 St John's Place
St John's Square
London EC1M 4DE
Tel: 071-490 7070

Yours (monthly)
Choice Publications (as above)

A magazine for the young at heart

Saga Magazine (monthly)
Saga Publishing Ltd
The Saga Building
Middleburg Square
Folkestone
Kent CT20 1AZ
Tel: 0303 857523

Retirement Planning and Living Magazine (quarterly)
MSM International
Thames House
18 Park Street
London SE1 9ER
Tel: 071-378 7131

The magazine of the Association of Retired Persons and the 050 Club. The 050/ARP Club members meet at different venues throughout the UK.

50-Forward
Freepost AT 180
The Manor House
46 London Road
Blackwater
Camberley
Surrey GU17 0AA
Tel: 0276 34462

Retirement Homes
available in larger newsagents

EIRE

Horizon (bi/monthly)
The Official Journal of the Retirement Planning Council of Ireland
16 Harcourt Street
Dublin 2
Tel: 01 783600

INDEX

127

129

MORE POSITIVE HEALTH GUIDES FROM OPTIMA

Positive Health Guides: 'A series that gives health education a good name.' *British Medical Journal*

Avoiding Osteoporosis by Dr Alan Dixon and Dr Anthony Woolf
Osteoporosis, or brittle bone disease, is the cause of pain and disability in one in four post-menopausal women in Britain. Yet this debilitating disease is preventable and treatable.

Dr Allan Dixon, Chairman of the National Osteoporosis Society, and Dr Anthony Woolf provide comprehensive and up-to-date information which is vital to all women and professionals concerned with the prevention of this disease.

Topics covered include:

- Causes and symptoms of osteoporosis
- Who is at risk
- Preventative measures during childhood, mid-life and old age
- Hormone Replacement Therapy and other treatments
- Practical guidance for safe and comfortable living

ISBN 0 356 15445 9
Price (in UK only) **£5.99**

Diabetes Beyond 40 by Dr Rowan Hillson
Diabetes Beyond 40 has been written specifically for people with diabetes who are in their forties or older. In detailed but simple terms the book covers:

- What is diabetes
- Looking after *your* diabetes
- Diet
- Exercise and relaxation
- Oral hypoglycaemics
- Insulin
- Blood glucose control
- Complications and prevention
- Self-help

- Enjoying everyday life

Dr Rowan Hillson, a Consultant with a special interest in diabetes at the Hillingdon Hospital Uxbridge has produced a comprehensive, informative and positive guide to the particulars of this disease as they relate to the older diabetic.
ISBN 0 356 14850 5
Price (in UK only) **£5.99**

Enjoy Sex in the Middle Years by Dr Christine E. Sandford

- Is your sex life as good as you want it to be?
- Do you no longer have time for sex?
- Is your relationship suffering as a result?

Dr Christine Sandford – a marriage guidance counsellor and adviser on sexual difficulties for over 20 years – offers reassuring and sympathetic advice on dealing with the worries that get in the way of a smooth and happy love life.
   'A valuable addition to the literature on sexual matters.' Dame Josephine Barnes, former President of the British Medical Council
   'This book will challenge many of the myths and old wives' tales.' Marriage Counselling Service, Ireland
ISBN 0 356 19673 9
Price (in UK only) **£5.99**

Beat Heart Disease! by Professor Ristéard Mulcahy
Coronary heart disease and stroke are widespread diseases whose incidence can be drastically reduced – simply by adopting a healthier lifestyle.
   Dr Mulcahy – a leading cardiologist – identifies the causes, key risk factors and typical danger signs and shows how to get back to enjoying life after a heart attack. Practical suggestions on how to modify your diet, change your lifestyle and take more exercise will not only help keep your heart healthy but bring you a happier and longer – life.
   'A splendid book to recommend to patients.' *British Medical Journal*
ISBN 0 356 19670 4
Price (in UK only) **£5.99**

The Breast Book by John Cochrane MS, FRCS and Dr Anne Szarewski
Recommended by the Family Planning Association
Every year thousands of anxious women consult their doctors about their breasts. Their anxieties range from suspected and actual lumps, premenstrual heaviness and tenderness, to dissatisfaction with their breasts' appearance.

Although the majority of breast problems are unrelated to cancer, and 80% of all lumps are benign, for most women the underlying fear is that they may have breast cancer.

The Breast Book, written by two specialists, aims to dispel anxiety by providing accurate and reassuring information. Illustrated throughout, the book covers

- The structure and function of the breasts
- The importance of self-examination
- Breast lumps and breast cancer
- Breast problems in pregnancy and breastfeeding
- Cosmetic and reconstructive surgery
- Breast problems and the Pill
- Psychological and emotional aspects

ISBN 0 356 15416 5
Price (in UK only) **£5.99**

The Menopause by Dr Jean Coope
The menopause is a normal event that faces every woman as her fertile years decline. For some it is approached with confidence, but for others it is a difficult time of transition and adjustment.

Dr Jean Coope, Family Planning adviser and Well-Woman counsellor with many years' experience researching the menopause, has written this invaluable and reassuring guide to coping with the 'change'. She answers many of the questions women raise on the menopause, and includes practical hints on:

- Keeping fit and healthy
- Avoiding osteoporosis
- Treatment for menopausal symptoms
- Continuing an enjoyable sex life
- Hormone Replacement Therapy

'Her practical hints for coping with "hot flushes" show Dr

Coope's talent for writing just what her readers really want to know.' *Doctor*

ISBN 0 356 14511 5
Price (in UK only) **£5.99**

Cervical Smear Test by Albert Singer FRCOG and Dr Anne Szarewski
Recommended by the Family Planning Association
Every woman who has ever been sexually active is at risk from cervical cancer.

The majority who develop this disease have never had a smear test, a simple procedure designed to detect pre-cancerous cell changes, which can be literally life-saving.

This fully comprehensive and illustrated book, written by two experts in their field, is designed to provide information about cervical smear testing pertinent to every woman, her partner and her doctor. It covers:

- What is a cervical smear
- What is a 'positive' smear
- What technical terms actually mean
- Colposcopy and its use
- Treating abnormalities
- Cervical cancer and its causes
- Viruses and cervical cancer
- Psychological and emotional aspects

ISBN 0 356 15065 8
Price (in UK only) **£5.99**

Get a Better Night's Sleep by Professor Ian Oswald and Kirstine Adam PhD

- Problems getting to sleep?
- Worried your sleep isn't as good as it should be?

In this practical and sympathetic guide, sleep experts Professor Ian Oswald and Dr Kirstine Adam help people with insomnia to achieve a more restful night's sleep. They identify the causes of broken sleep, insomnia and nightmares and show how nicotine and alcohol, poor diet, inadequate exercise and irregular hours affect the quality of your sleep. Their practical, scientifically based advice offers the best ways to avoid sleeplessness

and wake refreshed every morning.
'A riveting book for a non-medical audience.' *Observer*
ISBN 0 356 19674 7
Price (in UK only) **£5.99**

Stress and Relaxation
Relaxation is an excellent way of dealing with the stresses of modern life. Jane Madders, who has taught stress-management for over 40 years, describes in this book numerous relaxation techniques which can help everyone to counteract stress and lead a healthier life.

'This clearly illustrated book helps just about everyone of us, from the fraught parent, the irritated driver behind the wheel, the migraine sufferer to the insomniac, the older and maybe depressed person.' *Sunday Telegraph*

'Demonstrates expertise and a full competence with the relaxation techniques.' *International Stress and Tension Control Society.*

'A highly recommended book in the Positive Health Guide series outlining self-help ways to cope with stress.' *Good Health Guide.*
ISBN 0 356 14504 2
Price (in UK only) **£5.99**

All Optima books are available at your bookshop or newsagent, or can be ordered from the following address:

Optima, Cash Sales Department,
PO Box 11, Falmouth, Cornwall TR10 9EN

Please send cheque or postal order (no currency), and allow 60p for postage and packing for the first book, plus 25p for the second book and 15p for each additional book ordered up to a maximum charge of £1.90 in the UK.

Customers in Eire and BFPO please allow 60p for the first book, 25p for the second book plus 15p per copy for the next 7 books, thereafter 9p per book.

Overseas customers please allow £1.25 for postage and packing for the first book and 28p per copy for each additional book.